BRITISH CULT CINEMA

AMICUS TO ZARDOZ

BRITISH CULT CINEMA

AMICUS TO ZARDOZ

DAVID HARKIN

Matador
Unit E2 Airfield Business Park,
Harrison Road, Market Harborough,
Leicestershire. LE16 7UL
Tel: 0116 2792299
Email: books@troubador.co.uk
Web: www.troubador.co.uk/matador
Twitter: @matadorbooks

ISBN 978 1 80313 536 6

British Library Cataloguing in Publication Data.
A catalogue record for this book is available from the British Library.

Printed and bound by CPI Group (UK) Ltd, Croydon, CR0 4YY
Typeset in 11pt Josefin Sans by Troubador Publishing Ltd, Leicester, UK

Matador is an imprint of Troubador Publishing Ltd

For Golda and wee David

AUTHOR'S NOTE

British Cult Cinema: Amicus to Zardoz is an A to Z of British cult cinema, with each letter of the alphabet accorded a film title. Under the title "cult cinema", there should perhaps be the clarification that these films listed within fall under my own definition of the word "cult". The same can be said of the term "British", with some of the films listed perhaps not having an overtly British look. Indeed, *Zardoz*, mentioned in the book's title, is probably questionable. Although produced at Ardmore Studios and on location in Ireland, *Zardoz* is distinctly British to me. Maybe it's the pairing of a Scottish actor and an English actress, or it's the overall theme of the film; whatever the case, it just "feels" British. At times, the book may take a left turn and arrive at a debate on Brian De Palma or other American fare. Within the boundaries of film criticism, this may happen throughout the book. However, this is only a cursory glance, with the book aiming its cinematic guns firmly on British cinema.

There are, of course, many cult films that most cinephiles or indeed casual viewers would point to if comprising their own A-Z. As an example, *The Long Good Friday* or *The Wicker Man* are cult classics in their own right. But here, however, I have omitted such classics, with the view that *British Cult Cinema: Amicus to Zardoz* is a personal journey, for the most part; a space to reflect on films that may have travelled under the radar.

There is, of course, still room for a few Hammer horrors or a Hitchcock film or two, with Amicus Productions featuring significantly. As Amicus also features in the book's title, I think it's worth mentioning a few more words. I have the firm belief that an Amicus film is a quintessential cult film, with five Amicus films deserving their place in the main A to Z.

Amicus was spearheaded by two American-born producers called Milton Subotsky and Max J. Rosenberg. It was based at Shepperton Studios and most of their horror projects were grounded in a contemporary setting. A few of these more contemporary films appear within these pages. However, the genre most associated with Amicus is the anthology film. Because of the episodic nature of an anthology film, the two-man company were able to hire big stars for short periods of filming. In 1965, Amicus struck gold with their first anthology: *Dr Terror's House of Horrors*. An atmospheric mix of voodoo, vampires and werewolves, featuring the horror double act of Christopher Lee and Peter Cushing, it was, arguably, their crowning glory. Encouraged by *Dr Terror's* mass box office appeal, they returned to the anthology film time and time again, with *Torture Garden, The House That Dripped Blood, Tales from the Crypt, Asylum, The Vault of Horror* and *From Beyond the Grave*. Naturally, some of these are better than others, with *The House That Dripped Blood, Asylum*, and *The Vault of Horror* being personal favourites.

Amicus fell apart in the mid-1970s, with both Subotsky and Rosenberg going their separate ways. Subotsky continued the anthology tradition when he co-produced, *The Uncanny* in 1977 and the cult classic *The Monster Club* in the early 1980s. Both films have their fans, but it wasn't the same anymore. Amicus and their films have never left us and they remain very popular, regularly being shown on television.

During their heyday, Amicus gave Hammer, and any other horror company, a run for their money. In essence, their films are the definition of British cult cinema. The films listed in these pages range from Alfred Hitchcock's *Young and Innocent* in 1937 to Roger Moore's *North Sea Hijack* in 1980. During the 1980s and 90s, Hitchcock, Roger Moore, and Peter Cushing were never off the television. So, naturally, the films they left us get a mention. The book contains artwork by Robert Harkin, for which I am very grateful. I should also mention that the year noted for each film is the year it was released. This information has been largely taken from the DVD or source copy I viewed when compiling the book. Other books or journals may have films listed at slightly different running times. All the films reviewed, considered or mentioned in these pages was viewed in a European format at 25 frames per second, with the final running time rounded to the nearest minute.

So, with that out of the way, in closing, all I can say is if you have got this far into the book, it is my sincerest hope that you continue to read on and enjoy *British Cult Cinema: Amicus to Zardoz.*

David Harkin
July 2022

And Now the Screaming Starts!

"True vengeance on the house of Fengriffen"

Charles (Ian Ogilvy) and Catherine Fengriffen (Stephanie Beacham) arrive at Charles' family estate to begin their married life. Unfortunately for the two love birds, many years earlier, Charles's grandfather, Henry (Herbert Lom), chopped off the hand of a woodsman, and a family curse is set to ruin the newlywed's plan for a happy life together.

After having had massive success with a series of anthology films, Amicus produced *And Now the Screaming Starts!* in 1972. Essentially a gothic horror film, *And Now the Screaming Starts!* was filmed under the less than exciting but perhaps more suitable title *Fengriffen*. This was the preferred title of director Roy Ward Baker before producer Max J. Rosenberg changed it to the more commercial *And Now the Screaming Starts!*

The story begins with a *Rebecca*-style voiceover as Stephanie Beacham's Catherine rides up to the house of Fengriffen with Charles (Ian Ogilvy), her husband-to-be. Arriving at Charles's elegant stately mansion, Catherine somewhat prophetically enquires, "Is there a ghost?". Catherine finds an answer after Charles gives her a tour of the family portraits. Catherine's attention is drawn towards a painting of Charles's grandfather, Henry Fengriffen (Herbert Lom), when a sudden and bloodied hand bursts through the picture, frightening Catherine. This is a brilliant jump scare that anticipates George A. Romero's similar trick in the zombie classic *Day of the Dead*. There's a confusing rape scene involving Catherine and a severed hand (which supposedly embodies an evil family curse).

The severed hand is the same one from *Dr Terror's House of Horrors*, but that isn't what lets the scene down. It's just a bit too subtle and unclear; perhaps a drop of blood or something a bit more graphic could have helped things along. But, then again, Amicus, or indeed Milton Subotsky, was never about blood and gore. The film shifts up a gear when Catherine becomes pregnant, and everyone who knows anything about the family curse starts getting murdered. Maitland (Guy Rolfe), the family solicitor, gets an axe stuck in his head; Mrs Luke (Rosalie Crutchley), the housemaid, falls to her death, and the family doctor (Patrick Magee) gets strangled.

Around this time, Amicus regular Peter Cushing pops up as Dr Pope, helping to nudge the story in the right direction as we learn that Charles has a dark secret. Fifty years earlier, his grandfather, Henry Fengriffen, invaded the home of his servant, Silas (Geoffrey Whitehead), and raped his wife, Sarah (Sally Harrison). By Amicus standards, this rape scene is quite cruel and explicit. After the rape, Henry chops off Silas's right hand and Silas proclaims that "the next virgin bride to come to the house of Fengriffen will be violated" - hence the curse.

Even though it reeks of *The Hound of the Baskervilles*, the flashback to evil old Henry Fengriffen is the most shocking sequence that the film offers, with Herbert Lom excellent as the unpleasant and callous Henry. Geoffrey Whitehead plays two parts: Silas in the flashback and Silas's son in the rest of the film (also called Silas). Whitehead is gentle and innocent as Silas in the flashback, as well as being suitably scary playing the son. Silas Jnr. lives on the Fengriffen estate, his "perpetual right" for the rape of his mother by Henry Fengriffen.

OPPOSITE

***Stephanie Beacham as Catherine Fengriffen in* "And Now the Screaming Starts!"**

When Catherine overhears all this and everything else about the curse, it sends her crackers and she tries to stab her pregnant belly. Throughout the film, director Roy Ward Baker serves up similar shocks and scares. Yet, the climax featuring an axe-wielding Ian Ogilvy (which has a distinct echo of the actor's same antics in *Witchfinder General*) falls apart too quickly.

Director Roy Ward Baker's best ally is Stephanie Beacham playing the lady of the house. Beacham, adding a silent film nuance to her performance, is beautifully photographed by cinematographer Denys Coop. Dressed in beautiful period dress, she spends most of her screen time wandering around the house, exploring her new surroundings, and sharing some genuine onscreen chemistry with Ian Ogilvy.

The majority of Amicus's previous output had been placed in a contemporary setting, but with *And Now the Screaming Starts!* the company goes gothic and sets the film in 1795. Essentially, Amicus tried to play Hammer at its own game, but it only half worked. Maybe with a better ending or with a different title, the film would have been better remembered. In saying that, it bristles with gothic atmosphere, and Beacham, Ogilvy and Cushing are all very much worth watching. And at its most basic level, *And Now the Screaming Starts!* is an excellent exercise in cult horror nostalgia.

And Now the Screaming Starts!

Directed by Roy Ward Baker
Produced by Milton Subotsky, Max J. Rosenberg
Screenplay by Roger Marshall
Based on the novel "Fengriffen" by David Case
Running time: 90min
Colour
1973

The Beast Must Die

"Tonight, the beast must die"

Its Shaft meets the Wolfman meets Agatha Christie as a millionaire big game hunter invites a group of guests for a weekend away at his large estate, believing one of his guests to be a werewolf.

The Beast Must Die, the last horror film from Amicus Productions, kicks off with spoken subtitles informing us that "this film is a detective story in which you are the detective" before segueing into Douglas Gamley's waka-waka guitar score. Based on the short story *There Shall Be No Darkness* by James Blish, *The Beast Must Die* plays like a mash-up of Agatha Christie's *And Then There Were None* and Richard Connell's *The Most Dangerous Game*, resulting in a very entertaining British werewolf film.

Crazy millionaire Tom Newcliffe (Calvin Lockhart) invites a group of people to his house for the weekend, believing a member of his party to be a werewolf. Newcliffe's captive audience include Charles Gray as Arthur Bennington, a pre-Dumbledore Michael Gambon as pianist Jan Jarmokowski, Ciaran Madden as the clamorous Davina, Tom Chadbon as artist Paul Foote, with Marlene Clark as Newcliffe's wife Caroline, and Peter Cushing as Dr Lundgren.

Not all of Newcliffe's guests are happy with the situation, and in one of the weaker scenes in the film, Jan tries in vain to escape the madness. Chased by Newcliffe in a jeep and accompanied by a funky soundtrack, Jan and Newcliffe drive around in circles before the car chase abruptly ends with both men sharing a polite conversation. It's about as exciting as watching an old racing segment on *Grandstand*.

Much better is a helicopter chase, where Newcliffe riddles the countryside with bullets, although you would have to question Davina's assertion that "if it exists, Tom Newcliffe shot it". Dressed entirely in black leather, Newcliffe shoots plant pots, decimates a greenhouse, and even blows up a helicopter. Maybe killing the beast proves a little bit more elusive.

Calvin Lockhart gives Tom Newcliffe a lot of energy, perhaps too much, but his performance fits the film well. Good, too, is Charles Gray as Arthur Bennington who, in his inimitable style, gives us the best lines. Wearing a wonderfully wolfish hairpiece, Amicus regular Peter Cushing plays Dr Lundgren, an expert in werewolf mythology. Cushing delivers another centred, consistent performance, with the actor once again showing his skills in using props. One particular highlight, late in the film, is when the group finally determines who the werewolf is, with Cushing catching a silver bullet in his hand before cleaning the shell with his handkerchief. It is a simple bit of business, but it is executed with such style and movement. They didn't call him "Props Peter" for nothing. Marlene Clark, initially in a role possibly earmarked for Welsh superstar Shirley Bassey, plays Newcliffe's wife, Caroline. Clark, burdened with a poorly dubbed voice, is good in some early scenes but fades away until a pivotal scene towards the end.

Before we go on, *Legend of the Werewolf* is a less funky but functional British werewolf film from the 1970s. Unlike *The Beast Must Die*, it's a period piece set in Paris during the 19th century, with Peter Cushing as a kind of 19th century *Quincy*. Produced by the short-lived Tyburn Film Productions and directed by a jaded Freddie Francis with his son Kevin producing, *Legend of the Werewolf* is a lot of fun.

Anyway, back with *The Beast Must Die*. Amicus producer Milton Subotsky, impressed by Paul Annett's 1969 documentary *The Battle for The Battle of Britain*, promised to give Annett a chance to direct a film for Amicus. Annett, known mainly as a television director, would have to wait four long years to get his chance. When it did come with *The Beast Must Die*, Annett comes up trumps, with some skillful direction and excellent handling of his stellar cast. Annett had no idea that producer Milton Subotsky, during post-production, would include "a werewolf break", a segment where the film stops dead and a voiceover by Valentine Dyall informs us that we can guess who the werewolf is.

Director William Castle had used a similar gimmick in *Homicidal*, whereby a forty-second clock appeared onscreen, and cinema patrons were presented with a chance to leave the cinema if they were "too frightened to see the end of the picture". If any film deserved such a corny device, it's *The Beast Must Die*, and the sequence only adds to the films overtly 70s feel. Put simply, *The Beast Must Die* is a cast-iron classic. A must-see.

The Beast Must Die

Directed by Paul Annett
Produced by Milton Subotsky, Max J. Rosenberg and John Dark
Screenplay by Michael Winder
Based on the short story by James Blish
Running time: 93min
Colour
1974

Carry On Emmannuelle

"Thank you, Mrs Dangle, for a most unbelievable experience"

A British sex comedy that spoofs the sexploits of the Emmanuelle films while also providing the last hurrah for the original Carry On gang. Kenneth Williams plays a French diplomat whose wife, Emmannuelle (Suzanne Danielle), not being able to arouse her husband, fulfils her sexual passion with just about anyone whose interested.

It's 1978, and the 30th *Carry On* film, *Carry On Emmannuelle* (with an extra n!) dies at the British box office. The series had been needing CPR during the last few productions but with a lack of interest from the general public, a tired formula and changing tastes in the British film industry, the film, and the series as a whole, didn't have a chance. The series began in 1958 with *Carry On Sergeant*; this first film was coy, gentle and full of warmth, a trend that would continue for several films.

As the 1970s began, audiences flocked to the *Confession* films, not to mention such middle-brow fare as *Last Tango in Paris*. Suddenly, the *Carry On* films felt dated and out of touch. Producer Peter Roger's realised that the films had to enter the smuttier genre of the British sex comedy. In her single *Carry On* role, newcomer Suzanne Danielle plays Emmannuelle Prévert, a French ambassador's wife. While on a flight on Concorde, Emmannuelle begins to get frisky with Theodore Valentine (Larry Dann) and seduces him in the plane's toilet. Then, returning home to England, Emmannuelle, not finding enough sexual satisfaction with her husband (a tired Kenneth Williams), seduces everyone from her butler to a television host to an entire football team!

Parallel to these sexual encounters is Theodore, who has fallen in love with Emmannuelle, much to the annoyance of his over-protective mother (Beryl Reid). Having been spurned by Emmannuelle since their mile-high sexual encounter on Concorde, Theodore plans revenge by bringing Emmannuelle's sexual exploits to the attention of the national press.

The film is at its most successful when we visit the ambassadors' downstairs staff. Jack Douglas appears as Lyons, the butler, playing it straight and dropping his "Alf" character for the first time in his *Carry On* film career. Douglas had played it straight before in the television series *Carry On Laughing* in 1975 (as Lord Peter Flimsy), and you wonder if director Gerald Thomas had spotted the potential there. In the role of Lyons, Jack Douglas is excellent, particularly during the early part of the film. Good, too, is Kenneth Connor as chauffer Leyland. Back to his cockney everyman role of the earlier films, Connor gives the film some much-needed energy.

Indeed, when the downstairs staff reminisce about their most unusual romantic love affair, Leyland's vignette, featuring Clair Davenport as an adulteress old boiler, is one of the best sequences in the film. The scene is pure Benny Hill in its execution, but it has genuine laughs, generated by Kenneth Connor in his final big-screen performance.

At first, Kenneth Williams was not interested in appearing in the film and felt that the script was offensive. He requested rewrites, which were subsequently rejected, but an increased fee, and a car to chauffeur him to the studio bought his participation. As Emmannuelle's husband, he plays Émile Prévert and gamely goes through the motions once more for a twenty-sixth record *Carry On* film.

Carry On Emmannuelle has its fair share of detractors, and some of this criticism is fair. It tips more than a toe into the smuttier genre of the British sex comedy, and when it does, it feels out of place and, more than anything, else, feels a little desperate. But the death knell of the series had come two years earlier with 1976s *Carry On England*. This film featured mainly non-*Carry On* actors such as Patrick Mower and Judy Geeson with regular *Carry On* stars left to fill the more minor roles. Adding to this, *England* was without frequent composer Eric Rogers and went into production a week after the death of series cast leader Sid James.

It could be argued that by 1978, there was far too much carrying on for public consumption. *Carry On London* had a long run in the West End in 1974, followed by thirteen *Carry On Laughing* television episodes in 1975; not to mention a summer season at Scarborough with *Carry On Laughing: The Slimming Factory*, in 1976. Perhaps by 1977's compilation/celebration film, *That's Carry On*, the public appetite had considerably waned.

Conversely, however, *Emmannuelle* brings many *Carry On* stars back into more featured roles and gives them plenty of the film's funniest scenes. Joan Sims as Mrs Dangle has the best scene in the film. When asked to retell her most unusual romantic love affair, Mrs Dangle imaginatively tells her attentive audience how a simple laundrette is better than a pub to pick up a man. "Sometimes, when you least expect it, you see a stranger across a crowded launderette", on cue, some appropriate stripper music pipes up. And Mrs Dangle and a possible suitor (Victor Maddern) seductively reveal their dirty washing to one another. This sequence and the many scenes featuring Sims, Connors, Douglas, and Peter Butterworth are a great reminder of what a great comedy team the *Carry On* team undoubtedly was.

Yet, *Carry On Emmannuelle* tried to do something different, and it simply didn't work in the eyes of the critics or, indeed, the fans. The end of an era was in sight for a British institution, and it was coming fast.

Having said this, it was never supposed to be the end. Throughout the 1980s, there would be projects announced in the press that would have featured surviving *Carry On* stars spoofing hit television shows such as *Dallas* and *Neighbours*. Yet none of these projects came to fruition until *Carry On Columbus* belatedly and briefly, entered cinemas in 1992. *Carry On Emmannuelle* is by no means the best *Carry On*, but it is the most peculiar.

Carry On Emmannuelle

Directed by Gerald Thomas
Produced by Peter Rodgers
Screenplay by Lance Peters
(Uncredited Willy Rushton and Vince Powell)
Running time: 84min
Colour
1978

Dracula A.D. 1972

"A date with the devil"

Count Dracula (Christopher Lee) is at it again, this time with a bunch of annoying hippies. Doing what he does best, Professor Van Helsing (Peter Cushing) fights evil while trying to protect his granddaughter (Stephanie Beacham) from the Count's evil clutches.

In 1958, Hammer released the definitive film version of Bram Stoker's *Dracula*, while also making a star of Christopher Lee as the titular character, with Lee redefining the count for future generations. Therefore, it's surprising that when Hammer developed a follow-up (*The Brides of Dracula*) in 1960, only Peter Cushing returned, with Lee's Count Dracula replaced by another vampire, Baron Meinster (David Peel).

Fast-forward a decade, and in between *The Brides of Dracula* and *Dracula A.D. 1972,* several other sequels of varying quality were released, with *Taste the Blood of Dracula* the best of the bunch. *Dracula A.D. 1972* starts promisingly in 1872 with a struggle on the top of a runaway carriage. There's instant audience gratification as we see the first pairing of both Lee and Cushing in a Dracula film since their classic 1958 release. Soon, the carriage crashes, and Dracula dies after being impaled with the spokes from a wheel. As the titles begin, the action moves to contemporary London, and we get an assortment of bog-standard camera angles of 70s England. Barring a few sparse notes over the Warner Bros logo, we aren't treated to the return of James Bernard's classic theme but a more modern theme by Mike "*Manfred Mann*" Vickers. Worse is to come as we are introduced to a bunch of dancing hippies listening to the band *Stoneground.* Throughout this overlong sequence, the dialogue, the characters, and the music are so appalling that you're relieved when the scene, running at over six minutes, mercifully ends.

Unfortunately, the horror with the hippies continues, with everyone meeting up at a coffee bar called the Cavern. There's a discussion on "the new happenings" and a wish to do "something new, yet as old as time", with Johnny Alucard (Christopher Neame), a disciple of Dracula, persuading everyone to participate in a black mass at an abandoned church.

In terms of the cast, it's great to see Stephanie Beacham in a featured role as Jessica Van Helsing, but also embarrassing to see her deliver such clunky lines as, "Weird man. Way out". Screenwriter Don Houghton's dialogue in many exchanges between our young hippies is on a tightrope between being ludicrous and a hilarious parody of 70s hippie culture. Still, the film has much to recommend it; both Lee and Cushing are in top form. Lee has a terrific scene towards the end of the film when Cushing's Van Helsing tells a bloodthirsty Dracula, "Look on me and remember". Lee's terrifying reaction, his bloodshot eyes staring coldly back at Van Helsing, vividly recalls his debut as Dracula fourteen years earlier. Pushing sixty years old, Peter Cushing returns to the Dracula franchise and delivers a dynamic performance, appearing visibly quite agile. Late in the film, when searching for Jessica, Cushing quickly lifts his body weight to peer over a fence, and during a climactic battle next to a bathtub, Cushing's Van Helsing is more than a match for Johnny Alucard.

The church sequence at St Bartholph's is arguably the best scene in the film, as Johnny Alucard summons Dracula from the grave. The black mass has everything you'd expect from a 70s Hammer film: shaky camera work, the heaving breasts of Bond girl Caroline Munro, and more than a pint of blood. Dracula enters the scene with an excellent low camera angle with billowing smoke that ensures his malevolent presence over the rest of the film.

One regrettable and significant flaw in the film is that we have a film produced and set in 1970s London, with Dracula never venturing outside St Bartholph's crumbling walls. *The Satanic Rites of Dracula*, released the following year, would try to remedy the lack of locations and ultimately be an improvement on *Dracula A.D. 1972*.

The Satanic Rites of Dracula makes better use of locations in and around London, while also giving Christopher Lee a lot more dialogue. Peter Cushing returns as Van Helsing too and has his work cut out as the narrative follows a crazy story involving the bubonic plague. Joanna Lumley replaces Stephanie Beacham as Jessica, with the character being somewhat less ditzy.

Back with *Dracula A.D. 1972*, and the film gets going when the hippies start dying, and we are left with Cushing and a few dozy police officers on the hunt for Count Dracula. The combination of Lee and Cushing, Britain's most successful horror actors, is always worth watching but, if that is not enough, *Dracula A.D. 1972* is worth it just to hear Johnny Alucard say, "Dig the music, kids" when resurrecting Christopher Lee's Dracula for the penultimate time.

Dracula A.D. 1972

Directed by Alan Gibson
Produced by Josephine Douglas
Screenplay by Don Houghton
Running time: 92min
Colour
1972

OPPOSITE
Dracula A.D. 1972

The Earth Dies Screaming

"I thought you were dead?"

The earth is overrun by alien robots who turn their victims into blob-eyed zombies. To help save the world, American test pilot Jeff Nolan (Willard Parker) joins up with six other survivors in a bid to fight back and regain the planet.

Stock footage and some borrowings from the *Village of the Dammed* and 1964's *The Earth Dies Screaming* is off and running. Trains crash, planes fall out of the sky, and bodies litter the English countryside. Along with some distinct opening titles, accompanied by an eerie score by avant-garde composer Elisabeth Lutyens, *The Earth Dies Screaming* sets out its stall as a minor cult classic that still delivers some genuine shocks. Eight unnerving minutes pass by, all without dialogue, before the introduction of American import Willard Parker as test pilot Jeff Nolan. The screenplay's first uttering of dialogue happens when Jeff meets Quinn Taggart (Dennis Price) and Peggy Hatton (Virginia Field) in an introduction seething with underplayed melodrama. The mood changes, and with no apparent television and radio reception, our survivors casually sit around drinking whisky. Soon, after venturing outside, there's a call for more drinks as Jeff meets Edgar Otis (Thorley Walters) and Violet Courtland (Vanda Godsell).

OPPOSITE

***A scary visitor in* The Earth Dies Screaming**

the
EARTH DIES
SCREAMING

A discussion over a suspected gas attack is interrupted when Vi mistakenly spots what she thinks is the air force walking up the street. They may look cumbersome and barely able to move, but these extraterrestrial glass-headed robots kill Vi by mere touch when she runs out to the road and invertedly asks for help. It's a well-staged moment, aided by some practical use of framing and composition.

Adding to the drama and completing the group are Anna Palk as a pregnant Lorna and David Spenser as Mel - "Probably the most important people on earth right now". It soon becomes clear that these sluggish *Robby the Robot* knock-offs are not the only bad guys in *The Earth Dies Screaming*. In a plot development that would quickly become an entire genre of its own (thanks to George A. Romero), the recently deceased come back as sleepwalking zombies with "grey blobs" for eyes. This ominous development works well for the film and lands some real shock moments with the deadly robots and our boiled-eyed zombies stalking the English countryside. In a very successful sequence, director Terence Fisher and cinematographer Arthur Lavis create a terrific sense of danger when Peggy (Virginia Field) is trapped in a wardrobe, hiding from the walking dead. The scene builds and builds and is marvellously realised on a tight budget through terrific acting from the British-born Virginia Field.

Indeed, the acting throughout the film is solid. Willard Parker is very believable in the role of test pilot Jeff Nolan and, if anything, with the help of his American accent, widens the parochial feel of the film. The rest of the cast is good too, with Thorley Walters suitably kooky as Edgar Otis and Dennis Price well cast as the unfeeling and calculating Quin Taggart. *The Village of the Damned*, made a few years earlier, had also used the framework of extra-terrestrials visiting a small village. Starring an elegant, yet ageing, George Sanders, it all begins in the quiet village of Midwich on one particular afternoon with everyone falling to the ground. A few months later, the women in the village suddenly become pregnant. The newborn children grow at an incredible speed, sharing the same hair colour, the same strange hypnotic eyes, and an ability to read minds. Adding more menace to the pot, there are other such children elsewhere in the world, and they all must be stopped. *Village of the Damned* is a cracker of a film, filled with suspense, drama and solid performances.

Overall, *The Earth Dies Screaming* has a no-nonsense approach to its premise of a world in peril. However, perhaps due to the small budget, a more fitting title may have been *A Small Village in England Dies Screaming*. But, then again, a small budget and a small cast is one of the many reasons why the film is so memorable. Okay, the budgetary constraints mean the film can't help but feel slightly penned in, but that shouldn't make a big difference to your enjoyment of the film. If you fancy something in the wee small hours that's nostalgic yet still creepy, *The Earth Dies Screaming* may be worth checking out.

The Earth Dies Screaming

Directed by Terence Fisher
Produced by Robert L. Lippert and Jack Parsons
Screenplay by Henry Cross
Running time: 60min
B/W
1964

Frenzy

"You're my type of woman"

Bob Rusk (Barry Foster), the necktie murderer, stalks London's streets, slaying women as he goes. However, the police have their own suspect, Richard Blaney (Jon Finch), whose ex-wife Brenda (Barbara Leigh-Hunt) and current girlfriend Babs (Anna Massey) have been brutally murdered.

After the dismal *Torn Curtain* and *Topaz,* Hitchcock returned home, both figuratively and literally, with *Frenzy.* Unfortunately, since 1964s *Marnie,* Hitchcock's career had taken a disappointing turn for the worst since his golden period during the 1950s, where Hitchcock had directed such classics as *Rear Window, Vertigo* and *North by Northwest.* By the mid-1960s, after the release of *Psycho* and *The Birds,* it seemed as if Hitchcock was losing his touch. *Marnie,* viewed as a flawed masterpiece by some, was made by a director stuck in a time warp.

Still filming exteriors on sound stages, Hitchcock had to catch up with the "new wave" of French and Italian filmmakers who were making Hitchcock look like a dinosaur. Following the poor response to *Topaz* in 1969 - the second flop in three years - something had to happen. So, in a bid to return to form, Hitchcock returned to London. Although it was the London of 1971, he was returning to the London of his past. Hitchcock, son of a London greengrocer, set his new film *Frenzy* among the cabbages and carrots of London's Covent Garden. Based on Arthur La Bern's *Goodbye Piccadilly, Farewell Leicester Square, Frenzy* is Hitchcock's homecoming film.

Hitchcock had unsuccessfully tried to produce a similar film to *Frenzy*, under the name of *Kaleidoscope*, in the late 1960s. Unfortunately, only a few test reels survive, but it is apparent that this project would have been a departure for Hitchcock, with its use of natural light and proposed lack of stars. Indeed, *Frenzy* presents itself with no real stars; the actors were lifted from the London stage. None of *Frenzy's* cast equates with the sheer star power of Hitchcock's previous array of stars, such as Cary Grant, James Stewart and Grace Kelly.

In *Frenzy*, Bob Rusk (Barry Foster) is the "Necktie Murderer", someone so notorious that the screenplay draws our attention to Jack the Ripper and the then-recent John Christie murders. Our protagonist, and best buddy of Rusk, is Richard Blaney (Jon Finch), a divorced ex-RAF, soon-to-be-fired, barman. In typical Hitchcock fashion, Blaney is accused of rape and murder and is an innocent man on the run. Barry Foster plays Bob Rusk and, for the most part, is a likeable barrow boy. Indeed, Rusk is a much more likeable character than our protagonist, Richard Blaney. Barry Foster plays the role effectively - gone is the bumbling neurosis of Norman Bates. Rusk is much more animalistic than Norman Bates and is much more brutal than Bruno in *Strangers on a Train*. Jon Finch, fresh from playing the titular character in Roman Polanski's *Macbeth*, offers a decent performance in the central role of Blaney. Blaney, however innocent he may be, is a complicated character to like. In saying that, you still have to give the guy a chance!

The central set piece of *Frenzy* is the rape and murder of Brenda (Barbara Leigh-Hunt), the most shocking scene Hitchcock ever committed to film. When Rusk enters Brenda's matchmaking agency (The Blaney Bureau for Friendship and Marriage), the sequence begins with Rusk claiming to be looking for a particular type of woman.

Rusks claim that Brenda is his "type of woman", leaving her frightened and vulnerable. She tries to escape her ordeal with excuses that her "secretary may come back at any minute", which only makes Rusk angry, and it's not too long before her rape and murder are graphically depicted onscreen. Hitchcock wanted the scene to be even more graphic, with saliva and blood dripping from his victim's prolonged tongue. Fortunately, the audience is spared that disgusting image; however, what remains is a scene that is brutal and sadistic. *Frenzy*, unsuccessfully, tries to juxtapose this horror with droll humour, with Inspector Oxford (Alec McCowen) and his wife (Vivien Merchant) serving gourmet food. Their comedy double act is just too talky with too much narrative exposition and nothing of note that is either really funny or very memorable.

After two successive flops, Hitchcock wanted a hit and had sought playwright Anthony Shaffer's services. Hot after the long run of his play *Sleuth* in London's West End. Shaffer was just the kind of man Hitchcock liked (and needed) - a hitmaker. Henry Mancini, best known for *The Pink Panther* theme, had produced a sombre and very dark score for Frenzy before being replaced by Ron Goodwin's more celebratory score.

After all, this was a celebration. Finally, a return to form for Hitchcock and the smash hit he so willingly sought. The film has much to offer, including an array of British acting talent, such as Billie Whitelaw, Bernard Cribbins, Anna Massey and Barbara Leigh-Hunt. And there are some excellent sequences, such as the murder of Babs, featuring a famous tracking shot travelling down a staircase, or the celebrated potato truck scene, where Rusk tries to retrieve an incriminating tie pin. All in all, from the closing chapter of Hitchcock's career, *Frenzy* is undoubtedly my type of film.

OPPOSITE
Barry Foster as Rusk in Frenzy

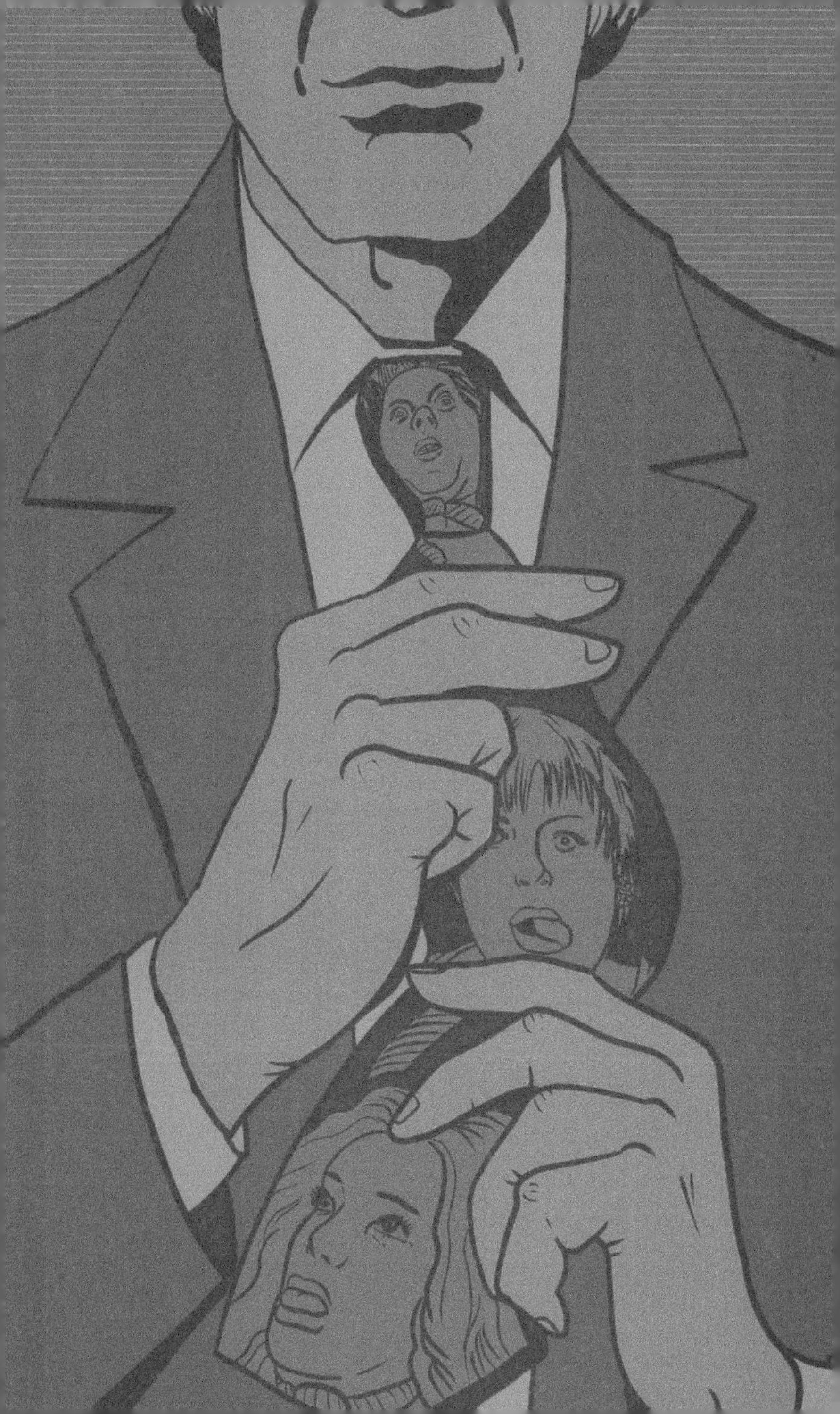

Frenzy

Directed by Alfred Hitchcock
Screenplay by Anthony Shaffer
Based on the book "Goodbye Piccadilly, Farewell Leicester Square"
by Arthur La Bern
Running time: 116min
Colour
1972

Gonks Go Beat

"If you're with it, you're in!"

Wilco Roger, the only space ambassador available in the galaxy, must create peace between two musical communities; one which enjoys rock and roll and another which only enjoys ballads.

In far-out outer space, a bemused Jerry Desmonde is unhappy over the continued bickering of two warring factions on planet Earth. Two groups of earthlings on two separate islands, so different, but wait for it, so groovy, they just don't get on! Their music styles are so different, they need a seemingly out-of-work Kenneth Connor to help sort out their disagreements.

Connor plays Wilco Roger, the only space ambassador on Jerry Desmonde's staff who is not on "space leave". In a prolonged and agonising cameo, Desmonde, as the "Great Galaxian", has little or no choice but to send Wilco Roger to planet Earth. In Beatland, all the groovy beat kids wear sunglasses, dress in trendy button-down shirts, and mime entirely out of sync to a horrendous song.

The song mercifully ends, and once your ears have stopped bleeding, Reginald Beckwith as The Professor, wanders around, telling one of the musicians that the next time he hears them play, he wants to "hear those big, big sounds that bring the coconuts down".

On Balladisle, there's another music lesson going on, as Wilco observes Derek (Charlie from *Casualty*) Thompson and his sister Elaine singing a pleasant ballad.

Two characters we never see again explain the threadbare plotline: "It's less than a week now until the Golden Guitar contest". And in a flash, Wilco meets Mr A&R (an embarrassed looking Frank Thornton), the man who oversees the contest. Mr A&R is first seen in shadow, and it's perhaps a shame that the director of photography never paid the same courtesy to Kenneth Connor and left the gifted comedy star in the dark. Mr A&R beckons Wilco to "gaze into the Golden Disc", and we are soon transported to a never-ending runway, where cars drive carefully up a depressing runway strip somewhere in England, presumably near the studio gates.

After gazing at the Golden Disc once more, we are transported to Balladisle to hear another obscure pop ballad. Wilco, worried that he will be exiled to Planet Gonk if he doesn't resolve the situation, decides that "love conquers all" and that the best course of action is to bring the two groups together with the help of *Romeo and Juliet*. Elsewhere, Steve (Iain Gregory) from Beatland is caught spying on Balladisle and is sentenced to twenty-eight days in the drum prison. The sequence in the drum prison isn't half bad, as a stream of talented drummers gives *Gonks Go Beat* its most pleasant piece of musicality. The only other musical entry to rival it is a bit later with Steve leaning on a rock crooning, "I just fell in love with you today". It's pleasing enough and shouldn't have you searching for the fast-forward button on your remote control.

Barbara Brown, providing a sweet performance as Helen, frees Steve from prison, with the pair joining forces while admitting to enjoying each other's taste in music. But, unfortunately, Helen's father, played by an enthusiastic Terry Scott, is under the impression that Steve has kidnapped his daughter. It leads the islands into war, a war that uses drumsticks as ammunition and guitars as weapons. Soon, however, Prime Minster Terry Scott realises that the battle was a mistake and that his daughter hadn't been kidnapped. Angry at the deception, Scott promises that his daughter Helen will never see Steve again. With the help of a goofy dream sequence, Wilko somehow decides that he has the answer to all of his problems. Then, through some intergalactic magic, Steve and Helen appear on stage at the Golden Guitar contest. They sing together, immediately bringing the warring factions together, allowing Wilko to return home and sparing him from a fate worse than death.

Kenneth Connor, who was on a five-year break from the *Carry On* films, gives a splendid performance as Wilko Roger. The actor was, if nothing, professional, and in *Gonks Go Beat,* he does what he can with the material at hand. *Gonks Go Beat* has some pleasing performances and some nice ballads if you have the patience to wait for them. The narrative may confuse some viewers, but then, *Gonks Go Beat* is a musical like no other. Released to a public who never asked for it and aimed towards a seemingly unknown demographic, *Gonks Go Beat* is a strange film indeed.

Gonks Go Beat

Directed by Robert Hartford-Davis
Produced by Peter Newbrook and by Robert Hartford-Davis
Screenplay by Jimmy Watson
Original Story by Robert Hartford-Davis and Peter Newbrook
Running time: 88min
Colour
1965

Hell Drivers

"Don't you characters ever say 'please'?"

Ex-convict Tom Yately (Stanley Baker) takes a job as a supply trucker at Hawletts, a road-haulage company, and begins a rivalry with Red (Patrick McGoohan), the head driver. A no-nonsense British drama with a stellar cast that included Sean Connery, Sid James, Jill Ireland, David McCallum, Wilfrid Lawson, Alfie Bass and Gordan Jackson.

Escaping his criminal past and on the lookout for work, Tom Yately (Stanley Baker) arrives at Hawletts, a road-haulage company run by the nasty Mr Cartley (William Hartnell). Tom finds a job as a short-distance driver and enters a world of corruption and brutality. Hawletts is a hotbed of tough-guy masculinity and childish pranks, with the drivers' time away from work consisting of late-night punch-ups and meals at a greasy spoon called The Pull In.

Tom meets another outsider, an Italian emigrant Gino (Herbert Lom), and strikes up an unlikely yet warm friendship. Herbert Lom's performance is terrific. In essence, Gino gives *Hell Drivers* its heart; his relationship with Tom is bittersweet and heartfelt.

At Hawletts, Cartley encourages his workforce to drive on "wet or fine" long country roads carrying ten tons of gravel, with each driver required to deliver at least twelve loads a day. The appropriately named Red (Patrick McGoohan) is the "pace-setter", with eighteen loads a day. If anyone can beat Red's record, a gold cigarette case worth £250 is waiting as a prize.

So, Tom sets out to beat Red's record while simultaneously catching the eye of a radiant Peggy Cummins as office worker Lucy. Lucy arrives "done up like a dog's dinner" at the village hall and only has eyes for Tom. Aware that Gino has romantic designs on Lucy, Tom's will is tested. Before there's room for any romance, the village hall becomes a barroom brawl when a fight breaks out with the locals. Tom takes no part in the fight, which alienates him from the other drivers.

Hell Drivers showcases an excellent fight between Red and Tom at the cashier's office. It's rough, bloody and savage - full of grit and authenticity for a film made in Britain in 1957. In the background, behind all the shenanigans at Hawletts, there's also a sobering backstory involving Tom's home life with his younger brother Jimmy (David McCallum). It's pretty grim stuff but handled well by Baker and McCallum and a clear juxtaposition from the raw masculinity seen elsewhere in *Hell Drivers*. Back at Hawletts, Tom learns that Red is in cahoots with Cartley, with both men pocketing money from the payroll. It all ends in a quarry with a tense and dramatic denouement for the snarling and bullish Red.

Behind the scenes, co-writer John Kruse based the script of *Hell Drivers* on his own experiences while driving lorries. These true-life experiences and some genuinely bleak cinematography by Geoffrey Unsworth help *Hell Drivers* gain a level of dark realism. Director Cy Endfield (credited as C. Raker Endfield), a refugee from communist witch-hunts in America, tips a wink at the French thriller *The Wages of Fear* and looks ahead to the more social realist work of the *Angry Young Men* generation.

Overall, *Hell Drivers* is a brilliant piece of filmmaking, with the supporting actors mainly taking up the roles of the other hell drivers, impressive too. Whenever *Hell Drivers* is discussed, it usually brings up the excellent trivia question: "What British film features...Inspector Clouseau's boss (Herbert Lom), James Bond

(Sean Connery), *The Prisoner* (Patrick McGoohan), *Doctor Who* (William Hartnell), a Professional (Gordan Jackson), and Sid James?" It's a fun question, but it does a disservice to *Hell Drivers*. Released in 1957, *Hell Drivers* has much to offer. It's a gritty slice of British filmmaking at its best, but, more importantly, it is a transitional piece, introducing a new kind of British actor.

The early part of the 1950s and most of post-war British cinema had belonged to actors such as Dirk Bogarde and Kenneth More, all hockey sticks and club ties. *Hell Drivers* looks ahead to the working-class careers of Richard Burton, Sean Connery and Stanley Baker. This change in audience taste and expectations is best illustrated in *Hell Drivers* when a train station clerk asks a bullish Tom, "Don't you characters ever say 'please'?"

Hell Drivers is a beautifully photographed, keenly observed character piece. More than a cult film, it's an excellent example of British cinema at its very best and it deserves your attention.

Hell Drivers

Directed by Cy Endfield (credited as C. Raker Endfield)
Produced by S. Benjamin Fisz
Screenplay by John Kruse and Cy Endfield (credited as C. Raker Endfield)
From a short story by John Kruse
Running Time: 108min
B/W
1957

The Intruder

"I'll help you to get away... if that's what you want"

Several years after World War Two, ex Col. Wolf Merton (Jack Hawkins) is now a successful businessman. However, the colonel gets his world turned upside down when he finds former army chum Ginger Edwards (Michael Medwin) robbing his home. Wishing to help his old friend, Merton is determined to find out why his old friend has turned to a life of crime.

Future Bond director Guy Hamilton directs this 1953 drama, which concerns ex-army soldier Ginger Edwards (Michael Medwin) and how his life changes from heroic wartime soldier to petty thief. The film kicks off with a clever shot: the camera travels along a line of tanks before settling on the ground when a stray golf ball falls beside one of them.

This framing and composition illustrate the two worlds that *The Intruder* reveals to us; the cosy middle-class world of golf-playing ex-Colonel Wolf Merton (Jack Hawkins) and the colonel's wartime past with a group of soldiers during battle. Returning home from his game of golf, Merton finds a man in his house. He realises that the intruder is ex-army pal, Ginger Edwards, who has fallen on bad times. Paranoid and edgy, Ginger is terrified of the police, while Merton wonders, "What's turned a good soldier into a thief?". The film steps up the action as we enter a flashback: on a battlefield, bombs blow billowing smoke and dirt into the air, and we learn that Ginger was a brave soldier during World War Two. We leave the flashback in the past and join Merton and Ginger in the present. Ginger makes a run for it and Merton, looking as if he's "seen a ghost", decides to help Ginger.

To do this, he visits another old army pal, John Summers (George Cole). This encounter leads to another wartime flashback, a sequence that reveals a theme that runs through *The Intruder,* that of the class struggle. Working-class John Summers gets a commission to become an officer. Yet Summers feels utterly ill at ease at the prospect, preferring instead to attend an out of bounds pub outside the grounds of his army base. Once there, he meets up with his cockney chum Ginger Edwards and both men enjoy a belly full of beer and a sing-song. Actor Dennis Price offers the film an excellent turn as Pirry, a snooty ex-officer who feels no compassion for his old army mates. The character of Pirry is best summed up during an exchange with Merton. When discussing his injury during the war and his lack of empathy for Ginger's journey into criminality, Pirry declares, "I could have cried with joy because I knew that I was rid of the whole stupid lot of you". It's a highly charged dramatic scene, made all the better by the fact we have already been made aware of how much of a cowardly officer Pirry was during the war.

The Intruder develops a slightly lighter tone as we enter another flashback involving Dora Bryan and Arthur Howard. Enjoying a tour of the inside of a tank, Dora Bryan plays Dora Bee, an unlikely pin-up, who shares some lighter moments with Arthur as the retiring Bertram Slake. However, it becomes pretty obvious that this is the calm before the storm as the best flashback is kept for the last as it focuses on Ginger coming home after the war. Set among the rubble of post-war Britain, it soon becomes evident that Ginger, if not a casualty of war, is a casualty of life. Still not out of his army uniform, he discovers that Tina (Susan Shaw), his bride to be, has found another lover.

Played with snake-like charm by Harold Lang, Bill, Tina's new lover, sits on a bed, ridiculing Gingers army uniform. Ginger,

OPPOSITE
The Intruder

disgusted and hurt, leaves Tina and Bill with the parting shot, "You can keep her". Even worse, Ginger's world is turned upside down with the death of his younger brother, Dickie. As a response to his uncle Walter's (Edward Chapman) past mistreatment of Dickie, Ginger gets a spell in prison after punching his uncle, leaving him at the bottom of a flight of stairs - dead.

It's a brief sequence, but it allows us, the viewers, a chance to see the screws getting turned and the transition between Ginger, the war hero, to the harsh realities of a life outside of the army, and how Ginger wound up in prison. Director Guy Hamilton keeps things ticking over well while also adding some nice visual and sound transitions, particularly when we go in and out of the many flashback sequences. Michael Medwin is superb in the central role of Ginger, revealing how a likeable young soldier can, when life gets in the way, become a thief and a thug.

In a role Jack Hawkins could have done in his sleep, he is in top form as ex-Colonel Wolf Merton. Overall, the acting throughout the film is of a high standard, with Jack Hawkins essentially acting as an anchor, bringing the many flashbacks and points of view together. *The Intruder* is a post-war drama that examines what becomes of soldiers once war has ended—a forgotten film, perhaps, but one that needs to be re-visited and re-assessed.

The Intruder

Directed by Guy Hamilton
Produced by Ivan Foxwell
Screenplay by Robin Maugham & John Hunter
Additional Scenes by Anthony Squire
Based on the novel "Line on Ginger" by Robin Maugham
Running time: 81 mins
B/W
1953

Jet Storm

"I am a lunatic. He made me so"

A scientist (Richard Attenborough), grief-stricken by his daughter's death, plants a homemade bomb on an aeroplane, aiming to kill one of the passengers.

In a forerunner of the disaster films of the 1970s, *Jet Storm* boasts an impressive cast of British actors, comedians, and even singing sensation Marty Wilde. The drama kicks off when Ernest Tilley (Richard Attenborough), overcome with grief due to his daughter's death three years earlier, boards a passenger plane flying from London to New York to exact his revenge on the man responsible. *Jet Storm* has a rather odd beginning, with Marty Wilde singing a melody over the opening credits; even more bizarre is that dear old Marty is singing "Jet stream, oh jet stream, please bring me home". Maybe Marty was breathing in too many jet fumes and had forgotten the title of the film.

Whatever the case, the film begins properly outside of an airport, with a cabbie ironically remarking, "Nice day for a flight, sir". With this scene, we get our first look at the best thing about *Jet Storm,* which is Richard Attenborough. As Attenborough would later prove with his role as John Christie in *10 Rillington Place,* he was more than capable of lending a character a dark, inner core. In *Jet Storm,* Attenborough is terrific, with his character driving the somewhat soapy narrative forward. On the same aeroplane as Tilley is James Brock (George Rose), the man responsible for the death of Tilley's seven-year-old daughter. Tilley confronts Brock in front of the other passengers, claiming that Brock, while driving drunk, had mounted a kerb, knocking his daughter over before then driving away.

Brock denies the allegations, claiming that Tilley is a "raving madman". Soon after, the other passengers onboard the plane begin to gossip about the possibility of Tilley having a gun. An intense Stanley Baker plays Captain Bardow who slowly calms the passengers down. When questioning Tilley, Bardow realises that it's not just Brock that's in danger, but everyone as Tilley has planted a bomb somewhere on the aeroplane. Throughout the cabin, the ensuing drama makes philosophers out of many of the passengers, with future *Yes Minister* star Paul Eddington believing that the ongoing situation is "God's justice" catching up with him in return for his adulterous behaviour.

If a film set on an aeroplane with a mad bomber sounds familiar - well, that's because it is. *Airport*, released eleven years later in 1970, has the same plot and bears many of the same characteristics as *Jet Storm*. The later *Airport* series of films boasted much more famous, if perhaps faded stars, but the set-up of a "soap opera" on wings remains the same. The first film in the series, *Airport*, has a mentally ill passenger who has hidden a bomb on board a plane. Starring a bored-looking Dean Martin opposite Burt Lancaster, *Airport* is a lot of fun and set the template for future instalments. Meanwhile, *Airport 1975* has a cocksure Charlton Heston trying to land a Boeing 747 after a mid-air collision. The series continued and improved with *Airport 77*, with Jack Lemmon, Lee Grant and Joseph Cotton all stuck on a plane at the bottom of the ocean. The last *Airport* film, *The Concorde - Airport 79*, featuring an intriguing musical score by Lalo Schifrin, is the silliest and probably the most enjoyable film in the series, as Robert Wagner fires rockets at a Concorde in a bid to silence a troublesome reporter. Unfortunately, this daft sequel spelt the end of the *Airport* series, but all four films are worth watching.

Back with *Jet Storm* and its stellar cast. Dame Sybil Thorndike, as Emma Morgan, sits with *Goons* star Harry Secombe as her cheeky comedy sparring partner for the entire journey. The Grande Dame of Shakespearean theatre is enormous fun in her scenes with Secombe, and these offer a respite from the sometimes overt melodrama onboard the Atlantic Queen. In a standout role as Mrs Satterly is brassy English actress Hermione Baddeley, who acts as a catalyst for much of this melodrama, with Diane Cilento and Elizabeth Sellars adding some much-needed glamour to the proceedings. *Jet Storm* has dated in parts; for example, today it seems odd that a commercial aeroplane flying from London to New York has only thirty-two people onboard! Still, the film has some tight editing, good use of music, and some nice byplay between the characters. And if you're a fan of disaster films, then sit yourself down and watch a black and white masterclass in melodrama.

Jet Storm

Directed by Cy Endfield (credited as C. Raker Endfield)
Produced by Steven Pallos
Screenplay by Cy Endfield (credited as C. Raker Endfield) and Sigmund Miller
From an original story by Sigmund Miller
Running Time: 87min
B/W
1959

Kidnapped

"I'll die for Scotland but not for him"

In Scotland, in 1746, after the battle of Culloden, David Balfour (Lawrence Douglas) is cheated out of his inheritance and nearly murdered by his greedy Uncle (Donald Pleasence). Sold as a slave, David meets up with Alan Breck (Michael Caine), and the pair become fast friends while sharing an adventure involving love, friendship and freedom.

A swashbuckling Michael Caine features strongly in this 1971 screen adaptation of Robert Louis Stevenson's 1886 novel *Kidnapped* and its sequel *Catriona*. The film follows the novel, and just as The Battle of Culloden ends in 18th century Scotland, David Balfour (newcomer Lawrence Douglas) visits his Uncle Ebenezer to claim his inheritance. In scene-stealing fashion, Donald Pleasence plays Uncle Ebenezer, who, when failing to have his nephew fall from a great height from the top of his dreary house, sells him to Captain Hoseason (Jack Hawkins).

Now kidnapped and on board a ship on the way to the Carolinas, young David is to be sold off as a slave. However, the situation improves when Captain Hoseasons' ship crashes into a small boat. David meets up with Michael Caine in the guise of Alan Breck, a character based on a real person but moulded as a swashbuckling Errol Flynn. Caine is splendid in the role, his Scottish accent a vast improvement on his American accent, with the cockney actor excelling in the many action scenes that follow.

After escaping from Captain Hoseason, David and Breck are indebted to one another with both men deciding to travel to

Edinburgh. Breck wishes to get a safe trip to France, and Balfour is hoping to "settle a score" with his Uncle for selling him off as a slave. The film switches gear when we meet James Stewart (Jack Watson) and his daughter Catriona (Vivien Heilbron). As a love interest in the film, Catriona and David make a cute couple. Scottish actress Vivien Heilbron adds a warmness to her role as Catriona, with the lush music score by Roy Budd helping their fledgeling romance. The story gathers pace when English soldiers arrive, headed by Mungo Campbell (Terry Richards). A shot rings out, and Mungo falls from his horse. Catriona's father, James Stewart, is wounded in the subsequent gun battle and is blamed for the murder of Mungo and brought to Edinburgh to stand trial.

Screenwriter Jack Pulman cuts out the second half of *Catriona*, leaving out David and Catriona's trip to Holland, and focuses on Balfour's attempt to stand as a witness in James Stewart's defence. *Kidnapped* has the added value of Trevor Howard as the Lord Advocate. Howard, figuring in just a few scenes, adds real creditability and class to the role. Unfortunately, the same can't be said of Freddie Jones, clearly not on his best form here as he adds unnecessary bluster to his scenes as clan leader Cluny MacPherson. In the central role of David Balfour, Lawrence Douglas is well-cast, adding a steely innocence to the part; it's just a shame that his screen career never really took off. *Kidnapped* has a richness and charm that separates it from a growing crowd of screen adaptations that populated the cinema in the early 1970s. On the face of it, the majority of the cast is impressive and solid throughout. And *Kidnapped* has some stunning cinematography by British stalwart Paul Beeson, filmed on location in Scotland.

Director Delbert Mann delivers a splendid adventure yarn, which could also be viewed as a statement on the futility of war. Mann begins the film after The Battle of Culloden, concentrating more on the victims than the battle itself, with much of the action that follows being depicted in a fast, snapshot style, allowing the narrative to be driven more by the characters and less by the swashbuckling antics of Alan Breck.

Alan Breck is the past, with David and Catriona the future. Breck, a victim of war and too many battles, looks upon the green fields and heather and remembers only the violence and the death he has witnessed. This view is best illustrated in an excellent montage towards the film's close, where we see Breck's thought processes: the endless violence, past battles, and his doomed future. Overall, *Kidnapped* serves up some imaginative storytelling, gentle romance and a sweet song during the end credits, sung by Mary Hopkin. All in all, if you're tired of the more recent, never-ending *Pirates of the Caribbean* franchise and need something a bit different, *Kidnapped* could be the answer you are looking for.

Kidnapped

Directed by Delbert Mann
Produced by Frederick Brogger
Screenplay by Jack Pulman
Based on the novels "Kidnapped" and "Catriona" by Robert Louis Stevenson
Running time: 103min
Colour
1971

The Land That Time Forgot

"Toward the greater mysteries that lie ahead of this land that time forgot"

After getting torpedoed by a German U-boat during WWI, Bowen Tyler (Doug McClure) and a crew of British seaman take a wrong turn and arrive on an island filled with dinosaurs and neanderthals.

Amicus producer Milton Subotsky had long wished to produce a film based on the work of American writer Edgar Rice Burroughs, creator of *Tarzan* and *John Carter*. And, after the disappointing box office and critical reception for *The Beast Must Die*, Subotsky got his wish when a film based on a novel by Burroughs went before the cameras in 1974.

The Land That Time Forgot is bookended with a bottle with a message floating in the sea. This device works well for the film, particularly at the beginning, as an old sailor picks up the bottle and reads the letter inside, allowing the story to begin. During World War One, a German U-boat torpedoes the merchant ship, the SS. Montrose. When the survivors of the Montrose gather together and share a flask of brandy, the U-boat surfaces, and the survivors spot an opportunity to board the U-boat and take it over, with tough-guy Bowen Tyler (Doug McClure) commenting, "It's the only chance we have". Tyler and the survivors successfully take over the U-boat, and a charming action-packed maritime adventure continues for about the next thirty minutes. This is all before Tyler realises that Lt Dietz, played by an ever-smirking Anthony Ainley, has placed a magnet beside the ship's compass, sending the U-boat south for six days.

The Germans momentarily take control of the U-Boat before biologist Lisa Clayton (Susan Penhaligon) gets something useful to do in the script and frees Tyler and the other survivors. Finally, the U-boat reaches the uncharted and fictional landmass of Caprona and, realising they're lost, Tyler reluctantly joins forces with German Captain Friedrich Von Schoenvorts (John McEnery). Once there, we find a lost world of dinosaurs and mumbling cavemen, with the island also offering an excellent supply of oil, which both the British and German crews must use to fuel their way home.

The stateside distributor for *The Land That Time Forgot*, American International Pictures, bagged Hollywood actor Doug McClure to play Bowen Tyler. McClure would carve out a career for himself in a string of cult films, including *Warlords of Atlantis, Firebird 2015 AD* and *Humanoids from the Deep*. In *The Land That Time Forgot*, McClure fills his role seamlessly, his tough American persona serving the film well, particularly in the many action scenes. 70s favourite Susan Penhaligon, unconvincing as a biologist, parrots token bits of information and is used mainly as set decoration. The script gives her little to do, even giving Captain Von Schoenvorts a more significant chunk of the biological gobbledygook.

Like *The Land That Time Forgot*, Amicus also released *At the Earth's Core*, another Burroughs adaptation featuring Doug McClure, albeit in a different role. *At the Earth's Core* tells the boring story of a giant drill, spinning its way to the earth's core, where McClure and a dotty Peter Cushing find a civilisation of primitive humans. More to the point. *The Land That Time Forgot* has a sequel, *The People That Time Forgot*, featuring wannabe movie star Patrick Wayne trying, in vain, to fill the Doug McClure role.

OPPOSITE

Fantasy meets action in The Land That Time Forgot

Sarah Douglas, best remembered for playing Ursa in the early *Superman* films, pops up too, as does David Prowse, Shane Rimmer and Thorley Walters. *The People That Time Forgot* kicks off when Major Ben McBride (Patrick Wayne) sets off in search of Bowen Tyler and meets his share of primitive creatures. If you can forgive *The People That Time Forgot* for not being as good as its predecessor, there is much to enjoy. Both films are a welcome reminder of a distinct style of filmmaking that involved cool special effects and "He-Man" heroics - a type of filmmaking that was quickly disappearing from view.

Behind the camera, *The Land That Time Forgot* has some shrewd trickery going on, with most of the attacking dinosaurs achieved through clever front projection and puppetry. Okay, within a few years, with the release of *Star Wars* in 1977, the effects would perhaps look dated. Nevertheless, they still have a charm and craftmanship all their own. *The Land That Time Forgot* remains a terrific blend of comic book adventure and Saturday afternoon matinee: perfect family viewing and perfect for anyone longing for the days before CGI.

The Land That Time Forgot

Directed by Kevin Connor
Produced by John Dark (Milton Subotsky and Max J. Rosenberg uncredited)
Screenplay by James Cawthorn and Michael Moorcock
Based on the novel by Edgar Rice Burroughs
Running time: 87min
Colour
1974

The Medusa Touch

"We are all the devil's children"

Violently attacked and left for dead, John Morlar (Richard Burton) lies in a hospital bed, wrapped in bandages. A French policeman reconstructs Morlar's life with the help of some journals and a psychiatrist and learns that Morlar has powerful telekinetic abilities.

The film begins promisingly as Inspector Brunel, a French detective on an exchange programme in London, is called in to investigate the apparent murder of John Morlar. Sergeant Duff (Michael Byrne), Brunel's English sidekick, enters the scene to examine the body. The police doctor states that Morlar's body "will spoil your breakfast". Then, suddenly, without warning, Morlar begins to breathe again and is rushed to the hospital. Next, the film steps up a gear as Richard Burton enters the film properly, as a string of clever flashbacks informs us about Morlar's "gift for disaster".

American actress Lee Remick who had been on similar spooky ground with *The Omen* two years earlier, plays psychiatrist Dr Zonfeld and shares some intense scenes with Richard Burton. Beautifully lit by Arthur Ibbetson, Remick turns in another strong performance with a surprising character arc. Author John Morlar (Richard Burton) is essentially an anti-establishment figure, believing that he can "do God's dirty work for him". Morlar's obsession with a scrapbook of recent disasters keeps Inspector Brunel on the case, as a series of flashbacks reveal the death of Morlar's parents and the incineration of Morlar's school, which leaves five people dead with Morlar believing that he "commanded it to happen".

The wreckage of a jumbo jet disaster hangs in the background of the narrative until a pivotal flashback in which Morlar reveals his telekinetic powers to Dr Zonfeld by mentally diverting that same jumbo jet into a tower block in central London. This sequence, bearing more than a passing resemblance to the real-life events in New York in September 2001, is served by some stunning model work and is very well executed.

In the role of Inspector Brunel, Lino Ventura's voice sounds dubbed, but his performance still shines, his lived-in face acting as a believable road map for a police detective's long career. Lino Ventura is in good company as *The Medusa Touch* is littered with stars in short cameo roles. Alan Badel, Michael Hordern, Derek Jacobi and Jeremy Brett all show up as day-players, with Harry Andrews and Gordon Jackson in more featured parts. Television supremo Lew Grade, the head of the production company behind *The Medusa Touch*, pulled a similar trick the same year with Raymond Chandler's *The Big Sleep*. Starring a weary-looking Robert Mitchum, this British version of the novel also featured a roll call of film stars in minor cameo roles, notably an elderly James Stewart.

Sharing some similar traits, released two years before *The Medusa Touch*, is the classic horror film *Carrie*. Directed by thriller specialist Brian De Palma, *Carrie* was the first in a long line of Stephen King stories that found their way onto the big screen and, on the whole, *Carrie* has some of the best jump scares in film history. The story follows Carrie White, a troubled teenager bullied by her schoolmates and generally misunderstood by everyone around her. Fortunately for Carrie, she has the power of telekinesis, and with it, she gets her revenge. Arguably the best sequence in the film is during the prom night finale. Expertly directed by Brian De Palma, the sequence is bloody, suspenseful, and rich in visuals.

De Palma followed up *Carrie* with another telekinetic narrative, the much-maligned thriller *The Fury*, in 1978. Psychic Robin

Sandza (Andrew Stevens) is kidnapped by evil bad guys who want to use his telekinetic powers for their political gains, and it's left to a craggy Kirk Douglas to save the day.

Back to *The Medusa Touch*, and television director Jack Gold adds some nice touches, such as adding a real-life newsreader to explain some background narratives. And the climactic destruction of the fictional "Minster Cathedral" is very well achieved, with some brilliant optical effects and sound design. Moreover, John Briley's screenplay has some excellent dialogue, primarily awarded to Richard Burton. *The Medusa Touch* shares some of the thrills and frills from the 70s disaster film craze and offers a towering performance by Richard Burton as author John Morlar, a marked improvement on his performance in *The Wild Geese*, released the same year.

Burton delivers a performance that is at one moment sympathetic and the next terrifying. It was certainly one of his best performances of the 1970s. Overall, *The Medusa Touch* is a well-designed thriller, overlooked in its day and deserving to be rediscovered and re-experienced by a new audience.

The Medusa Touch

Directed by Jack Gold
Produced by Anne V. Coates and Jack Gold
Screenplay by John Briley
Based on the novel by Peter Van Greenaway
Running time: 105min
Colour
1978

North Sea Hijack

"Well, he's either a genius or incredibly lucky."

Hired by the British government, Rufus Excalibur ffolkes (Roger Moore) must stop a group of terrorists who threaten to blow up North Sea oil rigs.

Roger Moore had scored massive success on television in the 1950s, 60s and early 1970s with appearances in *Ivanhoe, Maverick, The Saint* and *The Persuaders!* However, the actor had attempted to break away from his suave on-screen persona with *The Man Who Haunted Himself*, a film which he would later regard as his personal favourite. Fortunately for Moore, by the end of the 1970s, his television credits were now resigned to an optimistic Sherlock Holmes film (*Sherlock Holmes in New York*) produced for American television, the obligatory chat shows appearances and an all-singing appearance on *The Muppets*.

When *North Sea Hijack* was released in 1980, Moore had completed four James Bond films and had a string of other films to his credit. Mainly potboilers (*Gold, Shout at the Devil, Escape to Athena*), these films, scored moderate success at the box office but had reaffirmed the perceived notion of Moore being a Hollywood player. *North Sea Hijack,* written by Jack Davies (from his novel *Esther, Ruth and Jennifer*), was filmed on location in Galway, on the west coast of Ireland.

Davies, who had made his name as a screenwriter, was a neighbour of Moore's. Davies had asked Moore for his opinion of a script, then entitled *North Sea Ransom*. Moore, when reading the script, loved the main character of Rufus Excalibur ffolkes (with two small ffs) and lobbied to land the role. Rufus Excalibur ffolkes, a cat-loving, whisky-drinking counter-terrorism expert, is hired by the British government to stop a group of terrorists threatening to blow up oil rigs in the North Sea if their ransom demand of twenty-five million pounds is not met by the British government.

In the hands of Anthony Perkins, the terrorist leader Kramer becomes more than your average bad guy. Like Moore, Perkins was trying to get away from a role that was defining his entire career. It had been twenty years since his role as Norman Bates in *Psycho*, and the actor would resume the role a few years later in a series of belated sequels. In *North Sea Hijack*, Perkins manages to add a dynamic and captivating presence to the film, while also reminding audiences how vastly underused he had been as a performer in the latter stages of his career.

The story bounces between the crew of the stolen ship and the discussions between the British government on when to involve ffolkes and his team in resolving the situation, with ffolkes suggesting that "Kramer and his odious colleagues will be dead or disabled" before any bombs go off. English born director Andrew V. McLaglen had made his name in westerns, usually starring an ageing John Wayne, before moving over to more military fare. McLaglen was a skilled action director with a proven track record, yet *North Sea Hijack* has few action set pieces. At times, the film gets bogged down in talky, if somewhat entertaining, dialogue scenes.

Moore, sporting a full beard, has some good dialogue and witty exchanges with Jennifer Hilary and James Mason. Mason, a massive star on both sides of the Atlantic since the late 1940s, plays Admiral Sir Francis Brinsden who, essentially, becomes Moore's sparring partner in a war of words. There is also strong support from Lea Brodie as "sexy Sanna", and the casting of Faith Brooks as a female Prime Minister does not go unnoticed for a film produced in 1979.

Much in the same vein as *North Sea Hijack*, and directed by Andrew V. McLaglen is *The Wild Geese*. Released just before *North Sea Hijack, The Wild Geese* has the star attraction of Richard Burton, Richard Harris, and Roger Moore, all in lead roles. Burton, who stayed off the booze long enough to get the film made, plays Colonel Faulkner, who leads a group of mercenaries into Africa to rescue an African President. Essentially a boy's own adventure, *The Wild Geese* has a lot to recommend it and, if you ignore the dubious politics, is a lot of fun.

Back with *North Sea Hijack*, and the cinematography by Tony Imi is unfussy, while the music by Michael J. Lewis is functional and suspenseful when it needs to be. But it's Roger Moore's performance that's the winning ingredient; it's full of humour, vigour and grit. Unfortunately, *North Sea Hijack* did not perform well at the box office and was not well received by critics. Time, nonetheless, and a little perspective can give certain films another chance to find an audience and, certainly, *North Sea Hijack* deserves another opportunity to find you.

North Sea Hijack (also known as ffolkes)

Directed by Andrew V. McLaglen
Produced by Elliott Kastner
Screenplay by Jack Davies
Based on the novel "Esther, Ruth and Jennifer" by Jack Davies
Running time: 95min
Colour
1980

The October Man

"Nobody's safe with a man like that about"

After suffering a traumatic head injury after a bus crash, Jim Ackland (John Mills) becomes the prime suspect in a murder investigation.

The October Man, a post-war British mystery drama and the first film directed by Roy Ward Baker (credited as Roy Baker), is a forgotten film.

It features legendary British actor John Mills in the central role of Jim Ackland, with Joan Greenwood, Edward Chapman and Kay Walsh in solid support. In a captivating opening scene, Jim Ackland is travelling on a bus with a friend's daughter when it suddenly crashes, killing the young girl and leaving Ackland with a severe brain injury. So extreme is the trauma of the event, Ackland blames himself for the girl's death and attempts suicide twice. Starting a new life, he decides to stay at the dilapidated Brockhurst Common Hotel. An agitated Ackland meets the other residents and has difficulty adjusting to his new life. Finally, he finds a friend in Molly Newman (Kay Walsh) and shares a drink with her. Having such a keen interest in astrology, Molly names Ackland as an October man as "October people are affable, suave, dapper and have a sense of beauty". The story focuses briefly on Jim's fledgeling romance with Jenny Carden (Joan Greenwood) and, in the tradition of many films of the period, with the help of a montage, they are soon madly in love. Meanwhile, Molly, who had borrowed thirty pounds from Ackland, is found strangled. Knowledge of Ackland's head injury leads the hotel residents to be as judgemental as the police, and all concerned begin to suspect him of being the culprit. Suffering from his

continuing head injury, Ackland starts to wonder, "Perhaps I did kill her and don't remember".

So, let's get this out of the way. *The October Man* isn't so much a murder mystery as it is a romantic drama; it becomes pretty obvious who the killer is, even at first viewing. Although this doesn't matter as *The October Man* is a fascinating drama exploring post-war attitudes to mental health, with several characters treating mental illness as a catalyst for committing murder, with the screenplay littered with many derivative terms regarding mental illness. It seems as if a brain injury and some flimsy evidence gathered by the police is enough for guests at the hotel and the police to suspect Ackland of Molly's murder.

In the central role of Jim Ackland is John Mills, one of Britain's brightest post-war stars. Jim Ackland's sense of displacement, echoes a lost and depressing post-war Britain. John Mills screen presence and strong sympathetic performance help lift the story from the danger of becoming too over-the-top. Playing opposite to John Mills is smoky-voiced Joan Greenwood as Jenny Garden. Greenwood, who would find lasting fame for her masterful performance in *Kind Hearts and Coronets*, is, nevertheless, in *The October Man*, just plain average.

As Ackland's love interest, her role gets lost somewhere within the narrative. The part is somewhat one-dimensional, and the character seems to drift from one scene to the next. The other woman in Jim Ackland's life is Molly Newman, played by Kay Walsh, best remembered for her performance as Nancy in the 1948 adaptation of *Oliver Twist*. Molly's introduction adds a much-needed dynamic to the proceedings, with her strained relationship with hotel resident Mr "You used to be nice to me"

OPPOSITE
The October Man

Peachy (Edward Chapman) working well within the narrative. Perhaps best known for *A Night to Remember*, director Roy Ward Baker, for the most part, directs in a pedestrian and satisfactory fashion, with the bus crash at the beginning of the film his most successful sequence. Baker handles it brilliantly; the wintry exterior *mise-en-scène* is in stark contrast to the tender byplay between Ackland and the young girl inside the bus. The cinematography, the low-key lighting and hard shadows echo Jim's internal psychological plight. Produced during a time of classic British noir, the chiaroscuro lighting in *The October Man* is very effective, with the stark lighting adding a melancholy feel to the film.

Let's face it; *The October Man* is not held in the same regard as other more famous British films from the same period. It is, however, a fascinating post-war British psychological drama with a terrific centrepiece performance by John Mills. Of course, Roy Ward Baker would direct better films, and John Mills would perform in more prestigious productions; nonetheless, *The October Man* deserves better recognition.

The October Man

Directed by Roy Ward Baker (Credited as Roy Baker)
Produced by Eric Ambler
Screenplay by Eric Ambler
Running time: 91min
B/W
1947

The Punch and Judy Man

"But I'm not a strange man. You see me every day of the week"

Tony Hancock stretches his comedic chops as Wally Pinner, a Punch and Judy man, trying his best to survive the local government's snobbery in a small seaside town.

In the run-down seaside town of Piltdown live Punch and Judy man Wally Pinner (Tony Hancock) and his social-climbing wife Delia (Sylvia Syms). Joining Wally on the promenade is Charles "the Sandman" (John Le Mesurier), Nevil "the photographer" (Mario Fabrizi) and Edward (Hugh Lloyd), Wally's sidekick.

Wally and Delia have a strained marriage. Delia runs a small souvenir shop, while Wally and his assistant Edward spend their days on the beach, performing their Punch and Judy show. Delia wants more from life, and an offer from the Mayoress (Pauline Jameson) for Wally to perform at a gala dinner allows Delia to get a foot on the local society ladder. Wally, however, wishes to have nothing to do with the gala or the local council who run it.

Meanwhile, Peter, a small boy who watches the Punch and Judy show every day, has no money for his bus fare home. Wally finds Peter standing in a heavy rainstorm and decides to take him to the local ice cream parlour. This sequence with Peter (nephew to actress Sylvia Syms) devouring a Piltdown Glory ice cream and Hancock trying to keep up with his young friend is the best scene in the film - Hancock had never shown such tenderness before. Hancock had been riding the crest of a wave on radio and television during the previous decade with the hugely popular *Hancock's Half Hour*. Writers Ray Galton and Alan Simpson were the architects for this success, having virtually written every word Hancock had ever uttered on the BBC. Hancock hit the big screen with *The Rebel* in 1961. Released the same year as his final BBC television series, *The Rebel* was a great success. Soon after, Galton and Simpson began writing another feature film script, and then another, with Hancock simply rejecting each script.

In *The Rebel,* Hancock lives a dull and frustrating life. Jaded by his office job's daily routine and with his terrible sculptures and paintings underappreciated, he travels to Paris in search of artistic respect and appreciation. Once there, he soon finds a home, as beatniks and pseudo-intellectuals celebrate his dreadful artwork.

Released in 1961, *The Rebel* was a critical and commercial smash and should have been the beginning of a long and successful film career. However, due to Hancock's unsettled and troublesome personality, this was not to be. In essence, he was searching for international stardom and greater creative control. After Hancock had turned down so many ideas and scripts for future film projects, he and Galton and Simpson went their separate ways, with Hancock joining forces with poet and critic Philip Oakes to write *The Punch and Judy Man.*

The Punch and Judy Man could not have been more different than *The Rebel.* Audiences would have been startled by the change in comedic tone, not to mention the shift from colour to the stunning black and white cinematography by Gilbert Taylor. And, after having ditched his writers and the BBC, Hancock seems to have surrounded himself in a comfort blanket of his favourite actors. Hugh Lloyd, John Le Mesurier and Mario Fabrizi all returned from *The Rebel,* all with much more prominent roles. *The Punch and Judy Man* has several scenes laced with pathos, such as the discussion on marriage over a pot of tea with an earnest Charles remarking, "The lady said no" or the subtle opening scene over breakfast with Hancock and Sylvia Syms.

Hancock had always sought to find the reality or truth within any comedic situation, and with *The Punch and Judy Man*, the Birmingham-born actor gives it his best shot. Here, he discards his trusted homburg hat and astrakhan-collared coat (from his television programme), favouring a more authentic look. Hancock, no longer "the lad himself", had now transformed into a man with friends and a wife.

As Delia, Sylvia Syms is a delight and also made beautiful, under the lights of Gilbert Taylor. The rest of the cast is good too. Hugh Lloyd, who had featured heavily on the small screen in *Hancock's Half Hour*, is in fine form as Edward. In the role of Lady Jane Caterham, there is excellent support from Barbara Murray, at her snooty best, and John Le Mesurier offers a measured performance as the thoughtful Charles.

The Punch and Judy Man is not without its faults; the pie fight during the gala dinner escalates far too quickly and seems slightly misjudged, with everyone on the council becoming dramatically drunk all too quickly. Despite this minor error, *The Punch and Judy Man* is a flawed masterpiece and hopelessly promises what might have been, if only Hancock's film career, or indeed his life, had continued. If you are in the mood for a gentle, quiet comedy that observes social class, marriage, and friendship, you could do no wrong than by paying *The Punch and Judy Man* a visit.

The Punch and Judy Man

Directed by Jeremy Summers
Produced by Gordon L.T. Scott
Screenplay by Philip Oakes and Tony Hancock
Based on an original idea by Tony Hancock
Running time: 89min
B/W
1963

Queen Kong

"Him, we like for making Konga"

Kidnapped by film director Luce Habit (Rula Lenska), Ray Fay (Robin Askwith) gets chased through the jungle by a giant female ape. A comedy send-up of the classic 1933 film King Kong, featuring such 1970s sirens as Linda Hayden and Valerie Leon.

This 1970s effort from director Frank Agrama follows the original *Kong* quite closely, reversing the sex of the characters, with the damsel in distress now becoming a dude in distress. The filmmakers also choose to play around with some of the character names in *Queen Kong*, with original *Kong* actress Fay Ray becoming Ray Fay (Robin Askwith) and the lead actor from *King Kong*, Bruce Cabot, becoming Luce Habit. The film begins in the jungle, and after another failed screen test, film director Luce Habit (Rula Lenska) is desperate to find the right leading man for her new film project, remarking that "Somewhere, somewhere...there must be a man". Somewhere turns about to be 70s London and the right leading man turns out to be Ray Fay, played with great effort and enthusiasm by Robin Askwith. There's a short chase accompanied by sub-Benny Hill music as Ray Fay gets pursued through the Portobello Road for stealing a film poster (the original *King Kong* poster, no less).

When Ray Fay gets drugged by Luce Habit and taken onboard a ship called The Liberated Lady, the story segues into a 70s time capsule. A group of young women in crop tops and tight-fitting t-shirts sing about women's liberation, with the lyrics mentioning 70s icons Jane Fonda and Germaine Greer. Looking like something out of a *Matt Helm* film, the scene nevertheless suits *Queen Kong's* madness.

Of course, the lyrics and the entire routine are completely dated when viewed today, but in the context of British comedy back in the 70s, there was much more offensive content elsewhere.

Back with the film, and with The Liberated Lady arriving at Lazanga, an island "where they do the Konga". Ray Fay, Luce Habit, and the Liberated Lady's crew meet Valerie Leon as the Queen of the Nabongas. Continually chatting nonsense, the Queen of the Nabongas and her band of bikini beauties spot Ray Fay and readies him for a date with Queen Kong.

Buried in a massive cake on an enormous picnic table, Queen Kong arrives and takes Ray Fay on a tour of the jungle. Deep in the jungle, Queen Kong does battle with a couple of dodgy looking papier-mâché dinosaurs, and Queen Kong isn't too surprised when Ray Fay screams, "Help. It's a thingy!". Nevertheless, as Queen Kong becomes a star attraction, the action moves to London and, prefiguring *Airplane* by a few years, we get a singing nun (Linda Hayden) on a doomed aeroplane. All of this comes before we get presented with a climax involving Queen Kong on top of Big Ben, a painfully unfunny speech about feminism, and a jolly sing-song.

So, is *Queen Kong* any good? Well, the film needs to be re-watched to make sure that you are watching a comedy as there are some truly awful jokes. The performances are average, with both Richard Askwith and Rula Lenska trying their best throughout. However, some of Rula Lenska's dialogue seems to be fed through an interpreter, as most of it makes little sense.

It might be generous to say that *Queen Kong* has some cheap special effects. The shoddy model work is only equalled by the even more inferior rear-projection work and poor stock footage throughout the film. Still, Richard Askwiths onscreen efforts help move the film along, and you soon find yourself forgiving the film for its poor special effects.

Askwith had a pretty good career with a series of sex comedies, most notably the *Confession* films. A series of British sex comedies, which, while being popular at the box office, were loathed by critics, mainly due to their vulgarity and sexism. *Queen Kong* has less of the *Confession* films' vulgarity, but it's still entirely bonkers and barely got a theatrical release due to legal action by producer Dino De Laurentiis. He was making his own version of *King Kong*, and the ensuing legal action led to the staggering of *Queen Kong*'s release, burying the film for years. So, today, *Queen Kong* can only really be found on YouTube or on an expensive DVD release. But, let's face it, it's probably not worth buying a copy. *Queen Kong* is enjoyable in its own barmy way and, if nothing else, it's a slice of 70s nostalgia, well worth checking out.

Queen Kong

Directed by Frank Agrama
Screenplay by Fran Agrama and Ron Dobrin
Running Time: 84min
Colour
1976

Robbery

"This is the big one – the biggest"

After a successful diamond heist, Paul Clifton (Stanley Baker) leads a gang of crooks on an ambitious robbery. Clifton, however, has his work cut out as the police, led by Inspector Langdon (James Booth), are closing in.

The Great Train Robbery forms the basis of this 1967 British crime caper which features Stanley Baker (who also served as a co-producer) as crime boss Paul Clifton, a character loosely based on real train robber Bruce Reynolds. *Robbery* is a film with few distractions and centres most of its action on the build-up and execution of that famed robbery in August 1963. The film opens strongly with the theft of an attaché case full of diamonds and an ensuing car chase. This chase took eight days to film with some excellent camera work from Chic Waterson and solid location work. It would subsequently act as a calling card for director Peter Yates, who would direct the celebrated car chase in *Bullitt* in the following year.

After the car chase and the introduction of all of the leading players, the gang's next move is to use the stolen loot from the diamond robbery as seed money for their next big job. The gangs next job is the "big one" - the planning and robbery of a night train travelling from Glasgow to London. The actual robbing of the train follows the real events from the 1963 train robbery and is expertly filmed by director Peter Yates. The sequence is helped along with some tight editing from Reginald Beck and crisp photography from Douglas Slocombe. Lasting twenty-three minutes onscreen, the sequence is suspenseful and authentic. It

BANK OF ENGLAND
I Promise to pay the Bearer on Demand
the Sum of
TEN
Pounds
10

remains the best cinematic sequence that depicts those actual events from August 1963.

The events of the Great Train Robbery, as of 1967, had not yet been brought to the silver screen. However, under the title *Die Gentlemen bitten zur Kasse,* there had been a German attempt which was, in turn, re-edited for distribution as *The Great British Train Robbery.* This German effort is a difficult watch. Beginning with a dodgy voiceover, *The Great British Train Robbery* features a group of "Germanic cockneys" discussing and executing the robbery using jarring and badly dubbed English. In 1966, inspired by the robbery, *The Great St Trinian's Train Robbery* starred a miscast Frankie Howerd and the girls from the infamous school all mixed up in a dull crime caper. Released twenty-five years after the Great Train Robbery, pop star Phil Collins would star in *Buster.* This was a misjudged comedy/drama that romanticised the Great Train Robbery's criminality and is, perhaps, more famous now for the chart-busting singles from the soundtrack.

Robbery originally ended with Stanley Baker's crime boss Paul Clifton on a yacht with American actor Jason Robards. The suggestion was that an overlord had financed the train robbery and that Clifton and the rest of the gang were mere pawns in an altogether bigger plot. This sequence, when first viewed was dropped, as it looked ridiculous. The film now ends in the same way as its German counterpart, with a simple question mark. As the story did go on, this ending is much more satisfactory, with money and those responsible not found for years to come.

Frank Finlay, one of many in the impressive cast surrounding Stanley Baker, has a memorable role as Robinson. The gang spring Robinson from prison, only for him to then become a

OPPOSITE

Stanley Baker as Paul Clifton in Robbery

prisoner to the gang. This theme is best exemplified when Robinson has doubts about the robbery, with boss Clifton barking, "You're in", before locking Robinson in his car. Finlay is very effective in the role, with the character feeling out of touch with the rest of the criminal gang. His main desire is to speak with his wife once more. This desire, nonetheless, proves to be a threat to the gang as a poorly timed phone call from Robinson to his wife draws the police much closer to the gang.

In a central role, Stanley Baker is suitably cast as gang leader Paul Clifton. Acting as a linchpin, Baker spends much of the film explaining the plot while jogging in a park or standing next to an airport. Baker gives a commanding performance, lending gang leader Paul Clifton a real-world authenticity. Hot on the gang's trail is Inspector Langdon (James Booth). Langdon is a textbook detective with a dogged determination to catch the gang. Lumbered with the traditional traits of a TV detective, actor James Booth offers a solid performance and gets a good chunk of screen time.

However, elsewhere in the cast, *Robbery* has the rather pointless addition of Joanna Pettet as Kate. Pettet appears in a handful of scenes, seeming only to function as a second conscience for husband Paul Clifton, as well as giving the film a bit of sex appeal. Rarely getting an outing on the television schedules, *Robbery* is available on DVD and, in terms of suspense, action and style, it hits all the right notes: a cult film with a capital C.

Robbery

Directed by Peter Yates
Produced by Michael Deeley and Stanley Baker
Screenplay by Edward Boyd, Peter Yates, and George Markstein
Based on a treatment by Gerald Wilson
Running time: 110min
Colour
1967

The Saint's Return

"The Saint doesn't break the law; he just bends it."

After receiving a cable from an old girlfriend, The Saint (Louis Hayward) travels to London and gets involved in an illegal gambling racket.

Simon Templar, alias The Saint, sprang from the creative mind of author Leslie Charteris, and featured in a long-running series of books, television series, and several films, most notably the RKO second-features from the late 1930s and early 1940s. In the first RKO film, Louis Hayward became the first-ever person to play Simon Templar on the big screen with *The Saint in New York* in 1938. With this first attempt, Hayward's interpretation of Templar is a million miles away from the more widely viewed notion of Templar as a sophisticated, suave, modern-day Robin Hood. Instead, in this first film, Templar is no more than a thug with little or no charm.

After Louis Hayward departed the role, George Sanders played the role five times, interpreting Templar as a suave lounge lizard. In saying that, Sanders bags the best of the RKO films, with *The Saint in London* a clear winner. With the unlikely combination of big ears and a moustache, trophy-headed Hugh Sinclair took over the role from Sanders in two subsequent films (*The Saint's Vacation* and *The Saint Meets the Tiger*) with little success. So, after two uninspired films with Hugh Sinclair and after a decade away from the cinema. *The Saint Returns* (released as *The Saint's Girl Friday* in the U.S.) comes along, with the original Saint, Louis Hayward, returning after a fifteen-year gap.

After a short car chase, the film starts well when socialite Judy Fenton plunges her car into a river and dies. We get a stock shot of New York and a quick glimpse of Inspector John Henry Fernack. Fernack is delighted to learn that Templar is on a plane to London, and he sends his English counterpart, Chief Inspector Teal (Charles Victor), a cable reading "He's all yours brother". Having arrived in London, after Judy had sent him a cable asking for help, Templar is shocked to learn that she is dead. Templar is immediately suspicious and begins to investigate her death, stumbling onto an illegal gambling racket, with this particular racket picking its "suckers" and bringing them blindfolded onto a barge to gamble away their money.

Through a clever peephole, wannabe "Goodfella" Max Lennar (Sydney Tafler) immediately spots the Saint, and we get our first chance to see the steeliness behind Templar's suave exterior. Hayward is believable when pushing people about and gets a good fight scene when Templar duffs up some members of the "river mob".

Chief Inspector Teal tries, and fails, to keep tabs on Templar throughout these shenanigans, leading to some lighter moments that help brighten the gloomy narrative. Accompanied by a jazzy music cue, screen siren Diana Dors pops up, attempting to stall Templar as he searches Max Lennar's apartment for clues. This scene plays out particularly well, with action, comedy and sex all mixing well within the narrative. With the help of Hoppy (Thomas Gallagher), his part-time valet and bosom buddy, Templar tracks down the location of the gambling barge. Eventually, in the final reel, believing that Judy was "tied in with the gambling racket", Templar discovers the mastermind behind it.

OPPOSITE
Are you the famous Simon Templar?

The Saint's Return is atmospheric, fast-paced and funny in all the right places. There's even a clever twist at the end that comes as a pleasant surprise. With the exception of Thomas Gallagher in the role of Hoppy, the performances are strong too. Like Inspector Teal and Inspector Fernack, Hoppy is a Charteris original. But for me, his character is too annoying, and his inclusion in the films or television programmes never sits well. Ten years after *The Saint's Return,* Percy Herbert would play Hoppy alongside Roger Moore's Saint. And Herbert, just like Thomas Gallagher, would also prove to be annoying. Hoppy just seems too stupid to be a friend of the urbane and sophisticated Templar. *The Saint's Return* has some murky cinematography, but it has fine location work and solid direction by Seymour Friedman. Louis Hayward also gets his chance to put things right with his second go at playing Simon Templar. Okay, he may be slightly too old for the part, but he delivers - mixing the toughness of his earlier 1938 performance with a fresher, lighter approach. In short, Hayward's Saint is likeable, charming and dangerous.

In essence, *The Saint's Return* and Hayward's performance paved the way for Roger Moore's hugely successful television series in the following decade. Overall, this is probably one of the best Saint films, and if you get a chance to see it, you won't regret giving it an hour of your time.

The Saint's Return

Directed by Seymour Friedman
Produced by Anthony Hinds
Story and Screenplay by Allan Mackinnon
Based on characters created by Leslie Charteris
Running time: 65min
B/W
1953

The Terrornauts

"Hello earth, do you read me?"

Just as their science project's funding runs dry, a group of British scientists are transported to outer space where they meet an alien race intent on destroying Earth.

Future *Doomwatch* actor Simon Oates plays Dr Joe Burke and leads Project Star Talk, the main aim of which is to make contact with extraterrestrial life. Along for the ride are regular 60s television actors Stanley Meadows as Ben Keller and Bond girl Zena Marshall as Sally Lund.

Dr Burke is soon informed that Project Star Talk will run out of funding in three short months due to a lack of results. On cue, a faint signal from outer space is received by Dr Burke's team, kick-starting the story as we enter a cool flashback where Dr Burke reveals that when he was a little boy, he heard the same faint signal in a dream. It's pretty standard stuff, but the flashback sequence with an alien world with two moons and a strange black cube full of luminous crystals has an eerie fog of intrigue. Back in the real world and seemingly wandering in from another film, Joshua Yellowlees (Charles Hawtrey) is sent from the Holmes Foundation to review the enormous funds spent on Project Star Talk. Learning that Dr Burke plans to send a message back into outer space and possibly make contact with extraterrestrial lifeforms, Yellowlees screams, "This will cause a sensation!". It certainly won't get any laughs, as Hawtrey, best known as part of the *Carry On* team, gets very few opportunities to stretch his comedic muscles and merely tags along.

As an alien spacecraft transports everybody to another world, the complete lack of budget becomes evident as our travellers meet a noisy robot on casters. Looking like a design reject from *Forbidden Planet*, this intergalactic robot acts as a tour guide for Dr Burke and offers our space travellers a series of "intelligence tests". One such test is an encounter with a space creature with a misplaced eye and a giant claw.

The scene is all too brief, but it benefits from some pure nostalgic shock value. With its painted eye and visible dried glue, the monster itself is in keeping with the film's charm, and it is a shame that there is not more of the same.

Zena Marshall, who has spent much of the film nodding and agreeing with Dr Burke, falls on to a "matter transposer" and is transposed to an alien world. Dr Burke, accompanied by polystyrene rocks and mad savages in painted swimming caps, brings her back in a rare moment of heroism. There's a bit of business with Dr Burke attaching wires (sticking out from a swimming cap) into a black cube, while delivering such lines as "In the name of the people of the planet where I was born, a once-proud race...greetings". Maybe it should be Dr Berk instead of Dr Burke.

Produced by Amicus Productions, *The Terrornauts* followed on from Amicus's recent big-screen outings of two *Doctor Who* films: *Dr Who and the Daleks*, and the less successful *Daleks' Invasion Earth 2150 A.D.* Both films have their admirers and were armed with a bigger budget and, away from the confines of a BBC television studio, both films stand up well. However, *The Terrornauts* looks cheap. Produced on a meagre budget with special effects that would make Gerry Anderson blush, it is not in the same league as Amicus's two *Doctor Who* films.

A film in the same league as *The Terrornauts* and, perhaps, influenced by much better executed Hammer films of the 50s, is *They Came from Beyond Space*. This nutty Amicus film stars American actor Robert Hutton as Dr Curtis Temple, who is called in to lead a team of scientists when a strange formation of meteorites is discovered in a field in Cornwall. And that's not all; not only is Dr Temple a leading scientist but, halfway through the film, Dr Temple turns commando as he's also an expert in firearms and hand-to-hand combat. Horror veteran Michael Gough also shows up towards the end and looks suitably embarrassed.

Overall, *The Terrornauts* is full of surprises. Low budget specialist Montgomery Tully does what he can with the ropey effects, and science fiction writer John Brunner does an admirable job with adapting Murray Leinster's source material. Okay, some of the pacing and direction is sluggish, but it's a charming film from Amicus.

The Terrornauts

Directed by Montgomery Tully
Produced by Max J. Rosenberg and Milton Subotsky
Screenplay by John Brunner
Based on the novel "The Wailing Asteroid" by Murray Leinster
Theatrical version: 74min
Colour
1967

Unearthly Stranger

"Could I... or anyone... have held back the terror"

A British scientist (John Neville) working on a secret formula that can project a man to another world through the power of thought finds that his wife (Gabriella Licudi) is part of an alien army sent from outer space.

Distributed by Nat Cohen and Stuart Levy's Anglo-Amalgamated in 1963 and produced by *Avenger's* producer Albert Fennell, this second-feature, black and white effort carries on Hammer's pre-gothic period from the mid-1950s.

Starring future *X-Files* actor John Neville as Dr Mark Davidson, *Unearthly Stranger* tells the story of a British scientist working at the Royal Institute for Space Research. The good doctor's research is the theory that through the power of the mind and deep concentration, one can travel through space to another world.

The story develops more when Professor Munro (Warren Mitchell) suddenly dies after discovering a breakthrough in his research, and the newly married Dr Davidson soon finds himself with a job promotion. Taking up his new role, Dr Davidson is immediately put under suspicion by security chief Major Clarke (Patrick Newell) with the Major taking a keen interest in Julie (Gabriella Licudi), the doctor's new wife. Dr Davidson is defensive about any interest in his new wife but is aware of some unexplained behaviour, such as her inability to blink her eyes.

Dr Davidson also finds his wife to have no pulse and confides in his friend and fellow scientist John Lancaster (Philip Stone).

However, Professor Lancaster doubts Dr Davidson's observations. On the way to Dr Davidson's home, director John Krish plays around with the narrative, introducing Julia properly into the film, with some good use of sound effects, editing and dialogue.

Indeed, the screenplay is peppered with good dialogue, particularly with some clever lines referring to Julie as an "alien". Or when Dr Davidson is describing how he met his wife, adding, "this thing was staying in the same hotel, so we had breakfast the next morning". The way this dialogue is expertly weaved into Rex Charlton's screenplay with so much subtlety is one of the films many charms.

Back with the story. At Dr Davidsons' home, Professor Lancaster witnesses Julie using her bare hands to lift a hot casserole from an oven, alerting his suspicions that she is not who she appears to be. Adding fuel to Professor Lancaster's growing fears is Major Clarke's revelation that there is no record of Julie having lived anywhere before.

Even more bizarre, after a creepy scene at a children's playground which leaves Julie upset, the Major finds her at home with her tears melted into her face. Finally, all these threads come together in a well-worked climax, with Dr Davidson still needing some convincing that his wife Julie is from another world.

Unearthly Stranger is a well-executed second feature, helped along with a standout performance by John Neville. He was more a stage actor who had a sporadic screen career until Terry Gilliam cast him in *The Adventures of Baron Munchausen* in the late 1980s, which led to a late-career resurgence in the 1990s. In *Unearthly Stranger*, Neville offers a believable, grounded performance in an otherwise unbelievable storyline. Gabriella Licudi lends the story a convincing turn as the extra-terrestrial spouse. Licudi, with her exotic looks and accent, help ground the outer space narrative, as the audience can identify that Julia comes from "somewhere else". *Unearthly Stranger* benefits from the presence of stocky English-born actor Patrick Newell as Major Clarke, soon to be cast as "Mother" in *The Avengers*. Newell is superb in his role as the Major, being even more suspicious than the celestial Julie.

Elsewhere, in 1985's *Lifeforce*, there was another space girl from another world. This cult classic begins in outer space as a crew of astronauts find three floating humanoids and a bunch of massive bats. Naturally, the male crewmembers focus on the female humanoid, who also happens to be naked for most of the film. Back on earth, and with the astronauts seemingly all dead. The female humanoid, known as "Space Girl" (Mathilda May), strolls around naked, draining the "lifeforce" from anyone who gets close to her. At the time of its release, *Lifeforce* was scorned by critics and ignored by the public, with the original title "*The Space Vampires*" probably more fitting.

Unearthly Stranger is an intelligent, underrated film with a nice twist at the end and an eerie music score provided by English music pioneer Edward Williams. At a running time of seventy-six minutes, the film zips by with some great pacing and atmospheric cinematography. A great sci-fi film - not to be missed.

Unearthly Stranger

Directed by John Krish
Produced by Albert Fennell
Screenplay by Rex Charlton
Based on an idea by Jeffrey Stone
Running time: 76min
B/W
1963

The Vault of Horror

"Night after night, we have to retell the evil things we did"

Based on an EC Comic strip, five strangers share nightmarish stories as they sit together trapped in a basement.

One by one, five strangers enter an elevator in an office building somewhere in London. The men are surprised when the elevator takes them to the sub-basement, with a bemused Maitland (Michael Craig) pondering, "it looks like some sort of a club".

Next, all five men gather in a circle with Critchit (Terry-Thomas), remarking that the strange situation is "almost like a dream". Soon, everyone begins to discuss dreams, with the film entering the first of its many segments. The first story, Midnight Mess, begins things off as Rogers (Daniel Massey) searches for his sister Donna (Anna Massey). This segment flies by as *Randall and Hopkirk (Deceased)* star Mike Pratt turns up for about a minute, gets murdered, and all is revealed at a restaurant with a terrific mirror effect, dodgy-looking fangs, and some "tomato juice". The next segment, The Neat Job, is a lot of fun, as we find comedy icon Terry-Thomas as Critchit, a fanatical cleaner and organiser of "spaghetti sauce", who wishes everything to be in its place. South African-born Glynis Johns plays Critchits husky-voiced wife Eleanor and soon runs out of patience with her husband.

One of the best segments follows with This Trick Will Kill You, concerning a cynical magician searching for new tricks in India. A new rope trick fascinates Sebastian (Curt Jürgens) so much that he will do anything to get its secrets. Helped along with

some wizardry from the special effects department, this segment is memorable. Impressive, too, is Dawn Adams as the scheming Inez, helping to make the overall segment fun and spooky.

The following segment, Bargain in Death, sees science fiction star Edward Judd wasted and given little to do, as the narrative centres on Michael Craig and an insurance scam. This is the more comedic segment in the film, but not even a cameo from comedy cockney Arthur Mullard can save it from falling short. Famous for their roles on television in the *Doctor in the House* series, Robin Nedwell and Geoffrey Davies also feature "imaginatively" as two student doctors. Overall, Bargain in Death is a disjointed piece and a little disappointing. The final segment, Drawn and Quartered featuring a bearded Tom Baker, is the best and most violent segment. Baker, soon to be known as the fourth *Doctor Who*, plays Moore, an impoverished artist living on the island of Haiti. Swindled by a couple of art dealers, a voodoo curse is put on the swindlers by a Haitian witch doctor, and anything that Moore draws comes to life with devastating consequences. This piece is inventive, creepy, and well-edited; indeed, the entire film, regardless of which segment, benefits from some tight editing by Oswald Hafenrichter.

For any trivia fans, *The Vault of Horror* is the only Amicus anthology that doesn't feature either Christopher Lee or Peter Cushing. Rewind half a dozen years, and the pair featured in Amicus's first anthology film, *Dr Terror's House of Horrors*. As five men, each with their very own horror segment, enter a train carriage, *Dr Terror's* has a framing story that is a triumph in economy, quickly setting up our five main characters, as well as introducing the mysterious Dr Terror (or Sandor Schreck).

OPPOSITE
The Vault of Horror

In his element as the eerie Dr Terror, Peter Cushing deals out his tarot cards, with each member of his captive audience given their own spooky segment. The five stories play like a horror's greatest hits album; werewolves, creeping vines, voodoo, vampires, and a disembodied hand all make an appearance and all manage to entertain. Christopher Lee and Michael Gough feature in the best story. After being tricked and publicly humiliated, Lee plays a pompous art critic who runs over artist Eric Landor (Michael Gough). Eric, however, gets his revenge, or indeed his disembodied hand gets revenge, as it enjoys a good bit of screen time crawling around, seeking vengeance.

Back to *The Vault of Horror*, and Bargain in Death, could have done with a more substantial outline. Faking your own death to claim back the insurance money needs more screen time to get bedded in, and the massive close up of Michael Craig reading an edition of *Tales from the Crypt* is all too knowing. However, the Curt Jürgens segment, in which he plays a scornful magician in India, and Baker's vengeful artist, are excellent sequences, well worth the admission price alone.

The Vault of Horror was Max J. Rosenburg and Milton Subotsky's sixth anthology film and followed on from *Tales from the Crypt* and *Asylum*'s enormous success. However, following the release of *The Vault of Horror* in 1973, Amicus, and indeed the fortunes of other smaller British film companies, would suffer greatly in the coming years due to overcrowding in the horror market, lack of American investment and the box office clout of films such as *The Exorcist* and *The Texas Chainsaw Massacre*. These fresher, more horrific films, would change the landscape of horror cinema, leaving Amicus, Hammer, Tigon and everything in between, looking old-fashioned and out of step with audience expectations.

The Vault of Horror

Directed by Roy Ward Baker
Produced by Max J. Rosenberg and Milton Subotsky
Screenplay by Milton Subotsky
Based on stories by Al Feldstein and William M Gaines
Running time: 87 mins
Colour
1973

What's Good for the Goose

"I can't understand it. She behaved like a whore"

On his way to a banker's convention, Timothy Bartlett (Norman Wisdom) picks up two young hitchhikers and suffers a midlife crisis as he falls helplessly in love.

Norman Wisdom plays Timothy Bartlett, a middle-aged assistant banker bored with his life. While on his way to a banking conference in Southport, Bartlett picks up a couple of young female hitchhikers named Nikki and Meg, and he takes a particular liking to Nikki. Late one night at the Screaming Apple Discotheque, where British band *The Pretty Young Things* provides awful music, Bartlett arrives, conspicuous in his dinner suit among a crowd of groovy hippies. He meets Nikki once more and, seemingly, falls in love with her, or perhaps more correctly, falls for what she represents: the notion of being young and fun again.

What follows is a generation gap sex comedy, with an ageing Norman Wisdom taking the lead. Perhaps more famous for screaming, "Mr Grimsdale!", Norman Wisdom was cast in the same mould as Charlie Chaplin and had enjoyed a string of hits for the Rank Organisation, beginning with *Trouble in Store* in 1953 and ending with the largely unfunny *Pressed for Time* in 1966. Throughout these films, Wisdom would play his "Gump" character, a character Wisdom had developed on stage before making the transition to the silver screen in 1953. The Gump character wore an ill-fitting suit, cloth cap and would usually try to fulfil his romantic desires while playing the small man in a big world.

Yet by the 1960s, if audiences weren't tired of his films, Norman Wisdom certainly was. A public feud with the Rank Organisation by the mid-1960s, coupled with Wisdom's own desire to try different avenues of comedic creativity, led to a falling out. After a stint on Broadway, Wisdom returned to England. Back home and with his second marriage on the verge of collapse, loveable, family-friendly Norman Wisdom decided to reignite his British film career with a sex comedy.

What's Good for the Goose is a film, one could argue, which has very little sex and very little comedy. Regarding the comedic efforts, there are some enjoyable moments, such as Bartlett trying to smuggle Nikki into his hotel room or his interactions with Wisdom favourite David Lodge as a hotel porter.

These interactions are few and far between, but when they appear, they act as a reminder that Wisdom could still deliver the comedy goods when given some good material. Regarding the "sex" in this sex comedy, there is very little, unless one is interested in seeing the bare arse and pubic hair of a middle-aged Norman Wisdom. In the role of Nikki is a very young Sally Geeson, a few years off playing Sid James's daughter in Thames Television's *Bless This House*. In *What's Good for the Goose,* Geeson gives a cute and likeable performance. Geeson's warm comedic presence is a welcome addition to what is essentially a film about infidelity.

Infidelity and Norman Wisdoms onscreen persona are bizarre bedfellows. Wisdom's style of comedy by the late 1960s had got lost somewhere between the counterculture of raving hippies and Wisdom's cinematic star on the wane. This unlikely combination of changing times, and a career on the wane, leads to the main problem of *What's Good for the Goose.*

As a fan of Norman Wisdom, it's tough to watch Wisdom's Timothy Bartlett brazenly commit adultery. Bartlett chooses to forget (as does the narrative) his wife and three children. His affair is played out in a sordid romantic prism of trips to the beach and days at the fair. Undoubtedly, Wisdom was far more successful when playing the underdog, the little man with the world against him. Wisdom playing a selfish adulterer, with no thoughts of anything else but his mid-life crisis, is difficult to watch.

Adding fuel to this disappointment is the feeble direction by Cannon Group co-founder Menahem Golan, with the production feeling somewhat rushed and some scenes poorly blocked out. Perhaps even more troublesome is the last fifteen minutes of the film. After the affair with Nikki runs its course, the narrative takes on a strange turn when Bartlett invites his wife Margaret (Sally Bazely) to the same seaside town where his affair took place. With an unintentional echoing of Hitchcock's *Vertigo*, Bartlett dresses his wife up in clothes similar to Nikki, and it all gets a bit weird. Overall, the sequence is overlong, unfunny, but most of all sad. Before her transformation, Bartlett's wife, Margaret, all curlers and cold cream, is a boring nagging housewife. Her feelings, or even her knowledge of her husband's extramarital affair, are never explored.

What's Good for the Goose is bookended with a jaunty theme tune and sprinkled with some nice crumbs of comedy, but it is simply not enough. Instead, it's a generation-gap comedy that is mainly unfunny, and some of the blame must lie squarely at the feet of Norman Wisdom. Wisdom is given scriptwriting credits in the opening sequence and was mistaken to think that his core fan base would enjoy this new adventure into the world of the sex comedy. The failure of *What's Good for the Goose* drove Wisdom to pursue television roles and stage appearances throughout the 1970s and 80s, with the comedian only returning to the screen in 1992 with *Double X: The Name of the Game*. Cast in the improbable role of a safecracker. Wisdom is saddled with a confusing narrative and an incoherent climax.

Let down by poor writing, bad direction, and terrible editing; Wisdom had no place to hide.

If you're at all interested, *What's Good for the Goose* has a German version of the film available too. It shows more of Ms Geeson's perky breasts - but be warned, this German version still bears the same tired jokes. All in all, *What's Good for the Goose* is not one of Wisdom's best films or funniest, but it is undoubtedly his strangest.

What's Good for the Goose

Directed by Menahem Golan
Produced by Tony Tenser
Story and Screenplay by Menahem Golan
Script by Norman Wisdom (Dialogue by Christopher Gilmore)
Running time: 97min
Colour
1969

X the Unknown

"This thing can take up any shape it needs to"

A lump of radioactive mud runs amok in a Scottish village, with only American scientist Dr Adam Royston (Dean Jagger) able to stop it

After the tremendous success of *The Quatermass Xperiment*, Hammer's next sci-fi effort would be cult favourite *X the Unknown* in 1956. After the strings of James Bernard's terrific opening score have died down, the story begins at a gloomy gravel pit near Glasgow.

Gerald Gibbs' inky black and white photography helps set the scene as a group of soldiers with a Geiger counter find a mysterious radiation source under the ground. Suddenly, the ground appears to open, and an explosion from beneath the surface kills one of the soldiers (a pre-stardom Kenneth Cope). Fading American star, Dean Jagger, in the role of Dr Royston, is brought on to investigate and sets up camp near the explosion. An energy force from beneath the earth begins to take its form in a massive lump of glowing radioactive mud, with Royston suggesting that "the more it lives, the more it will grow". Before long, this lump of mud grows to an enormous size and begins a terrifying journey of destruction.

In essence, *X the Unknown* channels the fear of meddling with radiation while also acting as a social commentary on a post-war

OPPOSITE
Will the world survive?

Britain immersed in the paranoia of the unknown. This enemy from within premise was the brainchild of Hammer icon, Jimmy Sangster. Sangster, who had joined Hammer's parent company Exclusive in the late 1940s, worked with Hammer throughout the 1950s as a production manager and would soon become one of the architects of their glorious reinvention of the gothic horror film.

In 1955, Sangster was allowed by producer Anthony Hinds to pen the screenplay for *X the Unknown*, with Sangster adding an X in the title, fully expecting that the film would receive an X certificate by the British Board of Film Censors. Producer Anthony Hinds liked the script and readied it for production, with Sangster filling the roles of both production manager (a role he loathed) and writer on the film.

Joining Dean Jagger is a young Leo McKern as Inspector "Mac" McGill. Brought in to investigate the strange goings-on, Royston and McGill become fast friends, with Royston remarking that McGill is "one of my staunchest allies". Placed as an anchor to help explain (and dignify) the mumbo jumbo sci-fi is Dean Jagger. Jagger gives Royston unquestionable integrity as he treats the material with the right amount of respect and delivers dialogue that could sound ridiculous in someone else's hands.

X the Unknown has some fantastic special effects, particularly at the hospital when a staff member has his face melted. Headed by Hammer's special effects wizard Les Bowie, these dissolving effects are still scary, prefiguring the melting effects in Steven Spielberg's *Raiders of the Lost Ark* twenty-five years later. Another high point is James Bernard's film score, which adds a lot to the visuals, creating a memorable atmosphere.

Similar to *X the Unknown* in style are both of Hammer's early *Quatermass* films. *Quatermass 2* (a personal favourite) has Brian Donlevy reprising the role of Professor Bernard Quatermass from the first film, with Quatermass blundering into a plot involving a government project to produce synthetic food, with it soon becoming apparent that alien organisms have taken over any human, placing a jagged V-shaped mark on their body. Soaked in beautiful monochrome, Val Guest directs *Quatermass 2* in an assured cinéma verité style, with impressive (uncredited) matte paintings by Les Bowie.

Back to *X the Unknown,* and with the combination of great performances, and a terrifying music score, it has become a certified cult favourite. It has tight pacing, terrific special effects, a great ending and enjoyable performance by Dean Jagger. *X the Unknown* is an assured cult classic of Hammer's 1950s output, before their conveyor belt of classic gothic horror.

X the Unknown

Directed by Leslie Norman
Produced by Anthony Hinds
Screenplay by Jimmy Sangster
Running time: 77min
B/W
1956

Young and Innocent

"This woman has only been dead a few minutes"

Robert Tisdall (Derrick De Marney) finds himself accused of murdering a famous actress. And seeing no other option than to make a run for it and clear his name, he finds love and an unlikely friend in Erica (Nova Pilbeam), the Chief Constable's daughter.

In late 1936, Hitchcock and his frequent screenwriter Charles Bennett began working on *Young and Innocent* (renamed *The Girl was Young* in the U.S.).

Based on Josephine Tey's novel, *A Shilling for Candles*, Hitchcock's final screenplay would have little in common with Tey's story further than the first few chapters of the novel and a few character names.

Young and Innocent begins on a stormy night, during a tense argument between Christine Clay (Pamela Carme), a successful actress, and her husband Guy (George Curzon), a small-time musician with a twitch in his eyes. Christine is found strangled the following morning, washed up on a nearby beach, with the belt from a raincoat the apparent murder weapon. Missing his raincoat is Robert Tisdall (a sleepy Derrick De Marney), who had known Christine a few years earlier and who happens to see Christine's body washed up on the shore. Just as Robert runs off in the opposite direction to get some help, two female swimmers spot him and wrongly put two and two together.

Accused of her murder, Robert is brought to the local police station. When he hears that he is included in the dead woman's will, Robert collapses and falls to the floor. The police chief's daughter, Erica Burgoyne (Nova Pilbeam), brings the scene to life as she attempts to wake Robert up by twisting his ears, a trick she picked from "a boxers dressing room". Robert realises that his solicitor has no faith in his innocence and, wearing his solicitor's glasses as a disguise, he manages to get away. Later, he meets up with Erica when her car runs out of petrol in the middle of the countryside. Slowly, while Robert is in hiding in a mill, Erica falls for him when her initial stubbornness begins to flounder. The two join forces and decide to find Robert's missing raincoat, which they believe will clear him of any wrongdoing.

There follows the customary chases and punch-ups before it transpires that the killer gave the raincoat to a homeless man called Old Will (Edward Rigby). *Young and Innocent's* star is undoubtedly Nova Pilbeam. Three years earlier, Pilbeam had the relatively minor role of the kidnapped Betty Lawrence in Hitchcock's *The Man Who Knew Too Much*. Her role in *Young and Innocent* is similar to many of Hitchcock's future archetypal blondes but, perhaps, with less underlying sex appeal, no doubt due to the young actress's age. She had been in line to play the lead in Hitchcock's *The Lady Vanishes*, as well as having a chance to play the second Mrs de Winter in *Rebecca* in 1940, but none of these opportunities materialised. Nevertheless, her performance in *Young and Innocent* is strong, charming and, most of all, memorable. The story's denouement has the formal meeting of the two most important men in her life, her father, her moral compass, and Robert, her wild, youthful, and innocent lover.

Among the cast, there are solid performances and some often standout comedic performances, most notably in the party scene, with Hitchcock regular Basil Radford as Erica's Uncle (a scene American distributors would shamefully remove). Playing Erica's aunt Margaret, Mary Clare is delightfully sinister; it's just a shame that her role is so small. As the male lead, Derrick De Marney is no Robert Donat and, indeed, no Cary Grant but, then

again, he doesn't need to be. In *Young and Innocent*, Derrick De Marney does an admirable job within the confines of his role. And as the film plays out, you begin, like Erica, to fall for his charms and find yourself cheering him on to the final reel.

Young and Innocent has some extensive model work, and Bernard Knowles' cinematography, for the most part, is excellent, with some good use of location filming. However, some of the rear-projection work might be jarring for modern audiences.

Towards the end of the film, *Young and Innocent* features a bravado camera movement as the camera moves 145 feet across a ballroom, to where we finally see the face of the killer responsible for Christine Clay's murder. This long crane shot is perhaps the best-remembered sequence from the film and reportedly took two days to film, achieved by filming in Pinewood's largest sound stage (at that time). *Young and Innocent* distinguishes itself as the only one of Hitchcock's 1930s thrillers with no world politics or spy rings permeating the narrative. Instead, it is essentially a love story focused on the sexual politics between our two main characters and their quest for the truth. It's, without a doubt, worth a viewing, if not for its charm, warmth and humour, then for its anticipation of what Hitchcock had in store in the decades to come.

Young and Innocent

Directed by Alfred Hitchcock
Screenplay by Charles Bennett, Edwin Greenwood & Anthony Armstrong
Based on the novel "A Shilling for Candles" by Josephine Tey
Running time: 83min
B/W
1937

OPPOSITE

Young and Innocent

Zardoz

"Zardoz speaks to you, his chosen ones"

Zed (Sean Connery), one of the few intelligent exterminators in a crazy future dystopia, learns that Zardoz, the God, whom Zed must obey, is derived from The Wizard of Oz.

"I am Arthur Frayn, and I am Zardoz" (Niall Buggy) speaks a disembodied head in a confusing prologue that tries in vain to explain the bonkers plot of this 1970s cult classic. Once that's over, an enormous stone head moves slowly across the sky, landing in a field where a bunch of savages on horseback collect some guns. Everyone enthusiastically shouts "Praise be to Zardoz ", and a voice from within the head tells the savages that "the gun is good" and that the "penis is evil". Yes, it's this bad.

Burt Reynolds was reportedly due to play the lead character Zed but dropped out - maybe he read the script? Because it's pretty turgid stuff from the first few frames. Anyway, Connery, dressed in a red nappy and a long wig points a gun at the camera (possibly trying to shoot his agent), just before Beethoven's 7th symphony accompanies the title sequence. The large head takes off into the clouds, with Zed, inside the head, hiding under some grain. Coming out from beneath the grain and echoing the hand emerging from the water in *Deliverance*, Zed rises and shoots Arthur Frayn - who seems just to float away. Anyhow, the stone head lands in a place that looks strangely like County Wicklow in Ireland and, in contrast to *Deliverance's* masculinity, Zed finds a world run by females dressed in Grecian dress. This new world is the "vortex", where there's no death or new births and punishment is dealt by your body ageing; "They make you old, but they don't let you die", utters one of the inhabitants.

Zed learns of a world that mixes the old and the new, with a mill for making bread and a lost museum full of the great art of a world long forgotten. There's a veiled analogy concerning organised religion when Zed meets May (Sara Kestelman), and an embarrassing sequence when Consuella (Charlotte Rampling), one of the main gals in charge, attempts to arouse Zed with pornographic imagery, to find a link "between erotic stimulation, and erection". Perhaps Sean Connery should have just made another Bond film.

Connery's career by the 1970s was in the doldrums. Post *Diamonds Are Forever*, there were a few bright sparks with *The Offence* and *The Anderson Tapes* (both directed by Sidney Lumet), with Connery's biggest box office hits being ensemble pieces (*Murder on the Orient Express* and *A Bridge Too Far*). Yet, in 1976, *Robin and Marian* depicted a tired and bewildered Robin Hood (Sean Connery) who had fought long and hard during the Crusades and has returned home to Sherwood Forest. Arriving there, Robin meets all his old friends while also stirring up trouble with the Sheriff of Nottingham. Finally, Robin finds Marian, his lost love, and soon their romance is rekindled. Audrey Hepburn came out of retirement to play Marian, with Connery perfect as an ageing Robin Hood.

The supporting cast is impressive too, with Nicol Williamson as Little John and comedy legend Ronnie Barker in a rare screen outing as Friar Tuck. In a flawless performance, Robert Shaw, who had sparred so memorably with Connery in *From Russia with Love*, plays the Sheriff of Nottingham and shares a few sword fights with Robin's merry men. Director Richard Lester, helped by an exquisite score by John Barry, crafts a beautiful tale of faded youth, friendship and lost love.

With *Zardoz*, you get one long embarrassing film; it's a film where you need to be in the mood to watch it, presumably when there's nothing else to watch or when you're slightly drunk. There are plenty of ideas within the narrative and, perhaps, this is why the film fails - there are too many ideas. The idea of a fake God and the inability to die is interesting, as is the concept of Zed, the slave who becomes a saviour and can change the world. Yet these ideas are ruined by the film trying too hard to be provocative, trying too hard to be the next *2001: A Space Odyssey*.

Zardoz does have the saving grace of some terrific in-camera special effects and some stunning cinematography by Geoffrey Unsworth. Director John Boorman would carry on the confusion in *The Exorcist II: The Heretic*, and Sean Connery's career would soon bounce back after *Zardoż*, with the fantastic *The Man Who Would Be King* in 1975. Still, *Zardoz* is a must-see film, although for all the wrong reasons. With its mix of failed ideas and silly scenes, *Zardoz* may be the perfect cult film.

Zardoz

Directed by John Boorman
Produced by John Boorman
Screenplay by John Boorman
Running time: 102min
Colour
1974